History and Imperialism

History and Imperialism

Writings, 1963–1986

Louis Althusser

Edited and Translated by G.M. Goshgarian

polity

First published in French as Écrits sur l'histoire (1963–1986), © Presses Universitaires de France Humensis, 2018
This English edition © Polity Press, 2020

Polity Press
65 Bridge Street
Cambridge CB2 1UR, UK

Polity Press
101 Station Landing
Suite 300
Medford, MA 02155, USA

ISBN-13: 978-1-5095-3722-8
ISBN-13: 978-1-5095-3723-5 (pb)

A catalogue record for this book is available from the British Library.

Library of Congress Cataloging-in-Publication Data
Names: Althusser, Louis, 1918-1990. author. | Goshgarian, G. M., translator, editor.
Title: History and imperialism : writings, 1963-1986 / Louis Althusser ; translated by G.M. Goshgarian.
Description: Cambridge, UK ; Medford, MA, USA : Polity, 2019. | Originally published: Ecrits sur l'histoire, 1963-1986. Paris : Humensis, 2018. | Includes bibliographical references and index. | Summary: Writings on History brings together a selection of texts by Louis Althusser dating from 1963 to 1986, including essays, a lecture, notes to his collaborators, and the transcript of an informal 1963 discussion of literary history. These writings are concerned with the place of history in Marxist theory--Provided by publisher.
Identifiers: LCCN 2019024082 (print) | LCCN 2019024083 (ebook) | ISBN 9781509537228 | ISBN 9781509537235 (pb) | ISBN 9781509537242 (epub)
Subjects: LCSH: History--Philosophy. | Historicism.
Classification: LCC B2430.A472 E5 2019 (print) | LCC B2430.A472 (ebook) | DDC 194--dc23
LC record available at https://lccn.loc.gov/2019024082
LC ebook record available at https://lccn.loc.gov/2019024083

Typeset in 10.5 on 12pt Sabon
by Fakenham Prepress Solutions, Fakenham, Norfolk NR21 8NL
Printed and bound in Great Britain by CPI Group (UK) Ltd Croydon

For further information on Polity, visit our website: politybooks.com

Contents

Historicism is politics tailing history, the communists' politics tailing bourgeois history

Louis Althusser, Note in the margin of a draft of his 23 April 1976 presentation of his collection *Positions*

What is historicism, if not the philosophical expression of political opportunism, its justification and point of honour?

Louis Althusser, Letter of 28 July 1986
to his Italian comrades

Acknowledgements

G.M. Goshgarian thanks Nathalie Léger, director of the Institut mémoires de l'édition contemporaine, together with the rest of the Imec staff, and also François Boddaert, Jackie Épain, Luke Épain, Peter Schöttler and Laurie Tuller.

Note on the Text

by G.M. Goshgarian

With one semi-exception, Louis Althusser did not publish any of the texts on history contained in the present collection: four short notes detailing various aspects of his theory of historical time; his reply to a critique of his conception of the science of history by the well-known Marxist historian Pierre Vilar; a transcription of an informal discussion about the premises of a Marxist approach to literary history; a definition of historicism written at the request of a Soviet journalist and philosopher; the text of what seems to have been a course or public lecture on Marx and history; and, at the centre of the present collection, *Book on Imperialism*, a theorization of globalized capitalism that is also one of the founding texts of the Althusserian materialism of the encounter.

These texts are outlines and drafts; an informal talk posing as improvised remarks tape-recorded by happy accident; and notes on particular points reserved for a small circle of insiders. The manuscripts on which the versions presented here are based are all freely available in Althusser's archives, housed in the Institut mémoires de l'édition contemporaine (Imec) in Saint-Germain-la-Blanche-Herbe, near Caen, France. To judge by their physical appearance, 'Marx and History' is the only one of these writings to have been seriously revised. The manuscripts of the other eight hitherto unpublished texts collected here were very lightly retouched by their author, unlike most of the Althusserian manuscripts published posthumously in the last twenty-five years, a considerable number of which were so heavily revised that certain passages are hard to decipher. The reader will judge whether the fact that Althusser left these writings in a drawer is an indication of their insignificance. It may be left to the philosopher's biographer to enlighten us about the contingent circumstances of their genesis, about which I know next to nothing.[1] I content myself in what follows with providing basic information about the state of the manuscripts and the dates of their composition, adding, in the case of *Book on Imperialism*, a page or two on the type of publication for which Althusser seems to have intended it before consigning it to his files and, in the case of the reply to Vilar, a few words on the history of the unfinished dialogue between the two men.

The 'conversation' on the theory of literary history, which opens the present collection, is, more exactly, a monologue of over ten thousand words that is interrupted in three places by Althusser's unidentified interlocutor. Internal evidence shows that it dates from 1963, although Althusser himself dated the typed transcription to 1965 in organizing his archives. The tape recording has not been catalogued at the Imec and I have been unable to locate it, but this absence of an original is hardly cause for alarm: the document that stands in for it attests to an effort to reproduce Althusser's words with a fidelity so exact that it borders on fetishism. The words with which it begins, crossed out in pencil and therefore not reproduced in our edition, are proof: 'it's obviously pretty damned stupid to tape something of the sort without having prepared it beforehand' – a remark outside the limits of the text proper that rather too conspicuously advertises the improvised character of the reflections thus 'accidentally' preserved to be taken seriously. If the monologue that it prefaces suggests that Althusser's comments were in fact carefully prepared from start to finish and down to the level of detail, the coquettishness of this opening finds its extension in a certain carelessness of expression which, if it is inoffensive in oral discourse, can be irritating in a written text several pages long. While respecting the informal character of the text, I have therefore taken certain liberties in editing the transcription, eliminating a considerable number of repetitions, filler words, linguistic tics and so on. While waiting to see what the tape recording will reveal, if it is ever found, I have also ventured to correct a number of odd expressions that are probably attributable to errors of transcription, taking my licence from the fact that the infrequent corrections pencilled into the manuscript are not in Althusser's hand. When such editorial interventions are open to debate, they are put in square brackets and the reading found in the transcription is given in a note. Thus I have replaced 'c'est-à-dire un refus' [that is, a refusal] with 'a un statut' [has a status] and 'il [Roland Barthes] pense que le mot est dans la chose' [he thinks that the word is in the thing] with 'il pense que le beau est dans la chose' [he thinks that the beautiful is in the thing], while providing the rejected readings in a note. In contrast, I have not indicated that 'penser à un certain type d'histoire' [to think of a certain type of history] has been replaced by 'penser un certain type d'histoire' [to think a certain type of history]. I am also responsible for the division of the text into sections and for the section titles.

Nothing about the manuscripts of the four Notes calls for comment, aside from the rarity of the modifications that Althusser made to them. It is not clear when he wrote the Note that seems to be the oldest, titled 'Supplementary Note on History'. In it, he gives more precise explanations of aspects of the theory of historical temporality sketched in one of his two contributions to *Reading Capital*,[2] making it likely that he circulated this Note amongst his collaborators after recovering, early in 1966, from the depression that overcame him after the book they had co-authored appeared in autumn 1965. 'On Genesis', dated 22 September 1966 at the time of writing, provides a more detailed explanation, aleatory-materialist *avant la lettre*, of the same conception of the heterogeneity of historical time. This text takes its point of departure in a letter of Althusser's that has not been identified with certainty, but is most probably the one he wrote to René Diatkine on 22 August.[3] The manuscript of 'How Can Something Substantial Change?' (I have provided the title), dated 28 April 1970 at the time of writing, bears only one correction, of a typo; it looks like copy neatly typed up for the printer, which it most certainly was not, since publication of this short text in its day would probably have resulted in its author's expulsion from the French Communist Party at a time when he had plainly resolved to remain a member of it. 'On History,' dated 6 July 1986, was written in a trembling hand in a psychiatric clinic in Soisy-sur-Seine, near Paris. Along with 'Portrait of the Materialist Philosopher', it is one of Althusser's very last philosophical texts.[4]

'On Genesis' was recently published online.[5] The same is true of Althusser's projected reply to Pierre Vilar, probably written in 1972 or 1973. It first appeared in 2015, together with a downloadable version of the critique that precipitated it, 'Marxist History, a History in the Making: Towards a Dialogue with Althusser'.[6] Originally destined to take its place in a collection that Pierre Nora and Jacques Le Goff would publish in 1974, Vilar's critique was first published in the journal *Annales* at Le Goff's emphatic request,[7] as Vilar recalled almost fifteen years later in an interview testifying to the spirit in which Althusser wrote his reply.

> 'Marxist History' is not an essay directed 'against Althusser': it is an *attempt at dialogue with him*. I showed the manuscript to Althusser himself, who wholeheartedly approved of publishing it: 'Here we have the viewpoint of a historian', he told me; 'this historian is reacting to the accusation of having "lapsed into historicism" and he suspects me somewhat of "lapsing into theoreticism"; on the one hand, the philosopher, on the other, a practitioner of history; Marx is perhaps the only man who tried to be both: a useful discussion!' For my part, I pointed out, when Le Goff asked me for permission to publish the piece

in *Annales*, that this was the first time, as far as I knew, that Althusser's name would be appearing in print in the review, although the first thing everyone said to me, from Athens to Granada and from Lima to Berkeley, was 'tell us about Althusser!'. For a multidisciplinary review 'in vogue', this was puzzling (or all too easily explained).[8]

The dedication of the offprint of Vilar's essay, preserved in Althusser's archives, corroborates this testimony: 'For Louis Althusser, who has understood my intention in the kindest possible way, this "attack" that is in fact a common defence. Affectionately, Pierre Vilar.'[9]

Did Althusser leave the text of his 'projected reply' unfinished? Neither the manuscript's physical appearance nor its content proves it. Althusser may even have intended his short text to appear as such in the 1973 volume of *Annales*, as a companion piece to Vilar's critique. It should be added that, although the public dialogue between the philosopher and the historian failed to materialize at the time, it was initiated two years later during Althusser's habilitation at the University of Amiens before a large audience and a jury of which Vilar was one of the five members.[10] And nothing prevents us from discerning, in certain passages that Althusser wrote at the very end of his career amid the public silence that he had imposed on himself after killing his wife in 1980, a renewed attempt to enter into dialogue with the historian of 'conjunctural problematics'[11] – a dialogue that will have to wait for one of the 'posthumous encounters' that Althusser wrote about to bear fruit.[12]

The destiny of 'To Gretzky', which Althusser dated 20 January 1973 in his own hand, may surprise those who think that the Althusserian materialism of the encounter emerged in 1982–1983. In 1988, a version of the extract from this text included in the present collection was integrated into *Filosofía y marxismo: Entrevista a Louis Althusser por Fernanda Navarro*, the short book which announced, three years before his death on October 1990, the resurrection of the 'late Althusser'.[13] When it was translated into Spanish, the extract from 'To Gretzky' underwent a purely formal metamorphosis, with the result that its publication here cannot quite be called posthumous, although it is also impossible to affirm that the original was, properly speaking, published in its author's lifetime. In the 1973 version, 'To Gretzky' presents itself as the response to just one question, which a Soviet citizen by the name of Gretzky asked Althusser: 'What is to be understood by "historicism"?' In the 1988 version, certain affirmations in Althusser's answer have become questions, turning a professorial monologue into a lively exchange. Thus an observation of Althusser's in 'To Gretzky' – 'of course, absolute relativism is untenable (for, at the limit, one cannot even *state* it, as Plato objected)' – is put, fifteen years later, in Navarro's mouth, where it takes an interrogative turn: 'As a matter of fact, absolute relativism is untenable, is it not? Plato raised that objection; for, at the limit, one cannot even state it.' The exchange thus fabricated makes up *Entrevista*'s fourth and final chapter.[14] Since it was included neither in the French version of the Spanish interview published in 1994 in the collection *Sur la philosophie* nor in the English version based on the French,[15] it seemed to me worthwhile to present it to a French-speaking public in its original language and form and, now, to Anglophone readers. Like Navarro, I have not reproduced the latter half of 'To Gretzky', which is about Lucien Sève's humanist Marxism and structuralism considered as a 'spontaneous philosophy of scientists', for it contains nothing that Althusser does not say better elsewhere.

The evolution of the manuscript of 'Marx and History' is that of the typical unpublished Althusserian text. It saw three successive stages of development. The oldest state of the text, which is typewritten, bears a large number of handwritten corrections. They were integrated into a revised second version that was retyped and corrected by hand in its turn. The typescript of this second version was then photocopied and lightly retouched by hand, in order to end up in the folder from which it was retrieved forty years later. It is possible, however, that one of the versions of the text that was thus interred by its author found auditors, if not readers, a reminder that is an integral part of the typed text taking the form – 'read page *n*' – that Althusser generally used when he planned to quote, in a course or lecture, a passage that he did not want to write out. Dated 5 May 1975, this version of the text also bears, on page 1, a handwritten word that is hard to read, possibly the toponym Gien or Giens (or something else). This word disappears from the two later versions, as does the reminder 'read page 192', which is replaced by a bibliographical reference. Thus it would seem that 'Marx and History' is the text of a lecture that Althusser, at some point, prepared for publication in one form or another. I have based the present edition of this presumed lecture on the most recent version, which is also dated 5 May 1975, while reproducing, in the footnotes, the more interesting variants from the earlier versions.

The unpublished, unfinished book that dominates the present collection has its origins in a text called 'On Imperialism's Final Crisis', 'written in the train between Bologna and Forli the [blank space] July 1973', according to a note that Althusser scribbled at the top of one of the four handwritten versions of it. He filled in the blank later, dating these pages, which are hard to read, '9 July'. A letter that he wrote to Étienne Balibar ten days later, during a stay in Brittany, shows that he had already formed the project of turning this work-in-progress into the introduction to a short book, provisionally and inelegantly titled *What Is Imperialism? Toward Imperialism's Final Crisis*. The various chapters to which this book project gave rise materialized so rapidly thereafter that one can only assume that their author had already composed them mentally before committing them to paper. He suggests as much, in his fashion, in a letter that he sent Franca Madonia from Paris on 15 August: 'I have two or three things to write, of capital importance from a theoretical and political standpoint; I have them in my head.'[16]

By this time, he had already written, in the proper sense of the word, two of the ten chapters or sub-chapters that he would turn out before abandoning his project: 'On Certain Marxists' Relation to Marx's Work',[17] dated 14

August, and another, produced late in July, which has not been included in the present volume. Everything else in *Book on Imperialism*, as we have it, took form between 17 August, the date on which Althusser began writing 'What Is a Mode of Production?' and, probably, the end of the month, since what seems to be the most recent of the four versions of the prefatory text here entitled 'To my readers' is dated 29 August. Althusser submitted some of the chapters of his manuscript to the judgement of people close to him as soon as he had finished drafting them: Yves Duroux, Étienne Balibar, Emmanuel Terray, Hélène Rytmann, and perhaps others. Balibar, Terray and Rytmann, his companion, provided him with written comments that have been preserved in his archives. Terray's commentary, which is dated, confirms Althusser's own dating of the text.

These chapters were not revised in the light of the criticisms addressed to him. They exist in just one version that has undergone virtually no modification at all, aside from the countless changes that Althusser made while typing them. The same holds for all of the rest of the text. The manuscript on which the present edition of *Book on Imperialism* (the definitive version of the title he gave the text) is based is thus, for the most part, a hastily composed first draft, a 'book' which, thanks to its incompletion as well as the diversity of the problems addressed in it, looks more like a collection of essays, whose relevance to the question of imperialism does not, moreover, always leap to the eye. Althusser himself was well aware of the disjointed nature of the polemic that he was then rapidly drafting, a 'sustained volley aimed at all sorts of possible objectives', on his own evaluation of the first chapters, which he submitted to Terray's judgement on 19 August. At this stage of his project, he was even considering turning his text into two separate books, one of which, he wrote to Terray in the letter he sent him along with a photocopy of 'What is a Mode of Production?', would be 'very methodical and pedagogical' and also 'shorter' than the other.

He probably intended to include the 'pedagogical' book, at least, in a new series that the publishing house Hachette had recently suggested that he found – a suggestion that Althusser enthusiastically took up, in part because he was convinced that François Maspero, the publisher for whom he edited the series 'Théorie', in which his own texts as well as those of a considerable number of his collaborators had appeared since 1965, was losing momentum. The 'principle' informing the new series, 'Analyse', had been 'established' by the end of the summer, according to a letter that its future director sent to Renée Balibar on 28 August 1973. The books that would ultimately be included in it had been put on the drawing board much earlier: two of which Renée Balibar herself was the main author and a collection of essays by Althusser, *Elements of Self-Criticism*, the main text in which, the eponymous 'Elements of Self-Criticism', had been written in summer 1972, the other dating from June 1970.[18] The 'thing of such great importance on imperialism' did not have the time to join them in 'Analyse'.[19] A few months after *Éléments d'auto-critique* was published by Hachette in autumn 1974, this second and last Althusserian series was discontinued, essentially because its general editor refused, in January 1975, to pledge 'not to direct any book series, whether alone or in collaboration with others', of a kind that could compete directly with the collection 'Analyse' – in other words, because he refused 'to abandon François Maspero and turn to a bourgeois publisher', to cite the terms of several similar press releases diffused as early as October 1973 in, as Maspero put it, 'the provincial press under Hachette's control'.[20]

Did this publishing misadventure deal a fatal blow to Althusser's project to finish and publish *Book on Imperialism*? Or was it a casualty of the devastating depression, warning signs of which had materialized during, or in the form of, his frenetic composition of the text, forcing a 'slowdown'[21] in the last days of August before it caught up with him a month later and conducted him to a psychiatric clinic? Was it the aleatory-materialist heterodoxy of this text, which did not, in the end, much resemble a 'pedagogical' work, that made it inopportune to pursue the project after the philosopher had recovered in 1974? Was it the political risk he would have run in publishing the uncompromising attack which, springing from this heterodox materialism, was launched on the theory of imperialism that enjoyed the favour of the French Communist Party? Or had Althusser simply realized that his *Book* was so far from being 'methodical' that it had nothing of a book about it but the name, so that it would be wiser to revise and then integrate its different components into separate future works – a task to which he turned, in a sense, from 1975 on?

Whatever the reasons, Althusser left *Book on Imperialism* unpublished. In retrieving it from his archives forty-five years later, I have not attempted to impose on it the unity and coherence that it obviously lacks, except by excising certain chapters or sections which would most likely have been relegated to the 'short pedagogical book' destined for the 'Analyse' series – more precisely, for the political-theoretical sub-series of this series that was to be addressed to militants of the French Communist Party and other left parties and movements.[22] Let me say a concluding word about these chapters not included in the lightly abridged version of *Book on Imperialism* found below.

They are, first and foremost, those in which Althusser elaborates his refutation of the economic doctrine promoted by the Party leadership since the mid-1960s. Taking its point of departure or its pretext from a misinterpretation, as Althusser saw it, of Lenin's thesis that the capitalism of the monopolies and, consequently, imperialism, were the 'antechamber of socialism', this theory of 'state monopoly capitalism' constituted, he argued, a historicist perversion of Marxism and a theoretical rationalization of the reformism and opportunism that he had been combatting in his Party for the past fifteen years. If these passages of *Book on Imperialism* have not been included here, it is not because they have lost their interest in the age of 'globalization' – the opposite is the case – but, rather, in order to facilitate a project to bring them together with other unpublished writings of Althusser's bearing first and foremost on economic problems. While waiting for that collection, the reader will find an excellent summary of the Althusserian critique of the theory of state monopoly capitalism in his posthumously published *Les vaches noires: Interview imaginaire* (1976).[23]

I have also left aside a page on absolute surplus value, another on Gramsci's conception of hegemony and a text several pages long on the role of the sciences and technology in capitalism, because all three resemble notes rather than continuous texts. The introduction has also been excluded, because it is spread out over four overlapping versions that Althusser would no doubt have combined into one, but that I did not feel authorized to unify in his place. As for the prefatory text here called 'To my readers', I have reproduced the version that seems to be the most recent, leaving the others aside.

Slips of the pen and spelling and punctuation mistakes have been silently corrected. In particular, the capitalization of words that Althusser sometimes begins with upper-case and sometimes with lower-case letters has been largely standardized. Chapter titles have been put in brackets when they are not the author's, as have words inadvertently omitted in the manuscript.

[A Conversation on Literary History] (1963)

The question before us is that of a direct route, one that doesn't run through ideological obstructions, towards a problematic of literary history as such.

How can we formulate that? We can set out from a concept that's accepted, that's generally admitted, that is, the concept of literary history. We have two terms here: history and literary. We need to know what this type of history is and, if possible, what it consists of – that is, what the concepts that allow us to think and state it are.

The first thing is, obviously, to distinguish history from chronicle, because a chronicle isn't a history. We can say that most currently existing literary histories are disguised literary chronicles taking a real object as their alibi or pretext, which isn't, however, the object of history at the level at which literary history is in fact understood and envisaged by the one who produces it.

We can maybe even see that right away.

What is chronicle? It's a fellow who recounts events that have occurred. A chronicle is a narrative in which a fellow says: 'I was there and such-and-such happened and then something else did.' Or else he recounts what others have seen. In any case, a chronicle is a series of accounts, either the personal accounts of the one who's doing the narrating, or the personal accounts of witnesses whom he's heard and who have told him what they've seen. The basis for chronicle, when it's put in form, is chronology, time, *chronos*. ... The concept of a chronicle is the continuity of time – a continuity that is, moreover, more or less arbitrary, because in fact it's divided up. The time of witnesses is the time of ordinary life: it's the time of years, calendar time. It can also be the time whose rhythm is determined by a certain number of events considered essential for the individual involved. For example, he can superimpose the time of his own personal histories on the time of the calendar years – his wedding, his illnesses. (Now there's something one could do with Montaigne – find out what the superimposition of official time, everyone's time, on Montaigne's own time is – the time of the history of his voyages.)

That's the outer form of most classic literary histories. (I'm not talking about new attempts in literary criticism of the kind Richard and others are making.)[1] Someone recounts what has happened and the basic structure of the narrative is that of chronology, with specific rhythms, obviously, which can simply be the rhythm of the successive years or months or the rhythm of the major events in the life of the fellow telling the story. It's not in order to make a deduction from the chronicle of a psychological or biographical history of the fellow, but it's plain that there is a direct continuity between chronicle, literary history as chronicle, on the one hand, and literary history as an individual's literary biography.

The problem is the relation between what he writes first and what he writes later, whether there are early works and mature works, whether there are conversions and so on. But all that is in any case situated in a time about which one presupposes that it is a continuous time, the time of chronology – either outer, social chronology, or that which, in the chronology common to all men, corresponds to the chronology of a particular individual's biography.

On this one grafts – not necessarily by logical deduction, obviously, but by using external factors, external concepts, psychological or of some other kind – everything that can be called the basis of its ultimate concept, used by present-day literary history (I mean classic literary history), which basically consists in trying to account for an evolution by setting out from events punctuating the existence of an individual who, one fine day, started writing, writing, writing ... someone who is known as such, without reflecting on the fact that one is reflecting about an individual who is historically recognized as such. That is, one basically takes it for granted that everyone can become a writer and that the individuals who did are simply folks who were luckier than the rest.

That, moreover, is what allows the literary critic to believe that, with a little luck, he could have been the author he's commenting on. In fact, it's a great source of comfort to think that, basically, if Chateaubriand became what he was, it's because he was driven into exile, or if Flaubert became what he became, it's because he had a horrible childhood. Folks who had a happy childhood take comfort in that.

That's very schematic. By this means, however, by means of the biographical chronology of the author whose history the literary historian recounts, a kind of direct personal rapport is established between the historian and the writer whose history he recounts. They communicate directly, because they have [both][2] been born and because both of them began writing one day: the literary historian also began writing one day. So they find themselves in each other's company.

There's one small difference, however. It's that the writer writes better than the literary historian. And then they don't have the same object. That's a small difference that we'll have to account for.

Nevertheless, I believe that that is the common basis of the structure of the problematic in literary history. There can be a whole slew of variations: the individual's psychology or his psychological biography can be conceived in very different ways. With Guillemin, for example, one can look for all the scandals, more or less, in the belief that the secret of Rousseau's biography resides in the scandals.[3] Or else one can *not* look for them. One can simply confine oneself to such-and-such an episode. One can dig more or less deeply, one can plunge one's hands into a writer's guts or remain on the surface.

It has proved possible to change this too with the help of new psychological techniques, psychoanalytic concepts in particular. One would have to take a look at what Mauron does with them, because it's quite possible that Mauron's concepts aren't psychoanalytical[4] concepts, exactly ... because they're taken as concepts that can account for a biography.[5]

In that sense, psychoanalytical concepts are the equivalent of psychological concepts for these lads. When Mauron explains, bringing a certain number of psychoanalytical concepts to bear, that Mallarmé gave a line of poetry such-and-such a form, those psychoanalytical concepts are double-entry concepts or, rather, concepts with an entry and an exit. The entry is the fellow's life, it's what happened to him, it's a psychoanalytical interpretation of the fellow's biography. The exit is the presence of psychoanalytical structures in the fellow's literary comportment. It's not the same thing. Because, obviously, Mauron, in the case to hand, neglects something fundamental: the fact that all psychoanalytical comportments give rise to certain manifestations in all individuals, whereas only certain individuals' manifestations are considered to be aesthetic values.

I would say the following, then: we have, on the one hand, literary history, conceived with a certain conception of history as its bedrock. For when we talk about history, we need to know what we're putting into that word. At the limit, it's a conception of history as chronicle, that is, as chronology, which can then be, as chronology, either purely and simply the chronology of a fellow's literary productions or the chronology of his autobiography, with a search for explanations from that standpoint. Or else, at the other extreme, because this chronology obviously doesn't account for the fact that what's in question is a literary work, since the affiliation between the new criticism and its object is based on the fact that both are autobiographies and that they therefore have the same rhythm of development. The upshot is that one of them writes a work on which the other comments, but that the one who writes in order to comment on the work of the other will never be commented on in the way the first one's work is commented on.

Thus there's a [scale] of values between the two of them. The critic doesn't account for this difference in level. He has to look for a compensating factor and that, finally, is why every literary history that presents itself as chronology, perhaps psychological or even sociological chronology, must inevitably look for a compensating factor in a non-historical aesthetic – that is, in a theory of what is specific to the object of art or the literary object as such. The result is that we are inevitably referred to the other concept in the term 'literary history', to the literary as text, that is, the literary object, that which is responsible for the fact that a literary object isn't an object of everyday consumption. A literary object isn't a newspaper article or an advert for a scrubbing brush and so on. It's a good deal more dignified. So the theory of the specific difference of the literary object as such necessarily leads to an aesthetics.

In other words, in the classic conception of literary history, we necessarily have, first, a literary history with a conception of history that, basically, reduces history to chronicle. It's altogether incapable of accounting, at its level, for the fact that an individual, who leads a life like everyone else and who lives in a time that unfolds the way every other time does, becomes, at a given point in time, the author of a work that's called literary. On the other hand, we have a compensatory aesthetics; we have an extension, inevitably, in order to account for that which history as chronicle fails to account for.

This is philosophy's province. All literary history is necessarily accompanied by an ideology of the aesthetic, a latent or explicit ideology that is its obligatory complement. There isn't a single literary historian who doesn't, at some point, come to a halt before the aesthetic nature of the work of art as if before something sacred, [in order to] sketch a theory of it, whether he's a Platonist or a Hegelian or what have you. (In general, the Hegelians are a little more self-consistent, because they try to stick the aesthetic in history itself; most of the time, however, folks come to a halt before the sacred, the sacred monster that is the sheer fact of the existence of the aesthetic modality of the object they're studying.)

The sacred in question is, for example, the history of a god made man – this isn't a comparison, it's a concrete application. Well now: the sacred commences from the moment of birth. The historian of aesthetic literature as such encounters his object's aesthetic modality from the moment of its birth. Hence a whole aesthetics of aesthetic creation. It's more or less 'little child will grow up if God gives him life'. Since the little child is God Himself, he gives himself life. So that continues, which is to say that once he's born, he develops and has misadventures of all sorts, he experiences all sorts of misfortune, including the passion. [And then] it's all over. And all that is aesthetic.

In other words, we have aesthetic categories – aesthetic creation, aesthetic passion, aesthetic suffering, aesthetic death. This aesthetic pseudo-history is never anything other than the projection of aesthetic categories, that is, of an ideology of the aesthetic whose traces the literary historian looks for in the sensuous history of the world, like the theologians who look for the trace of Christ, of God made man, in the concrete history of humanity.

This happens in the Old Testament, in the Near East and so on. Why does it happen there? That's just the way it is and that's all there is to it. The problem re-appears the other way around: Why is it that what is sacred about the aesthetic, the aesthetic as such, happens to find itself incarnated on such-and-such a day in such-and-such an individual, who, one fine day, in a trance, became the site of an aesthetic creation? Why doesn't the milkman next door also have a right to aesthetic creation?

Plainly, all this presupposes that there are folks who have a rapport with this world of aesthetic reality as such, who excel for reasons we don't really know, simply because they are in fact writers. That is to say that the fact that they are writers is absolutely not thought [*réfléchi*].

The Aesthetic as Structure: Roland Barthes

This aesthetic can itself be the object of different variations, different sets of themes [*thématiques*] and so on. In any case, its basic presupposition is that it is something aesthetic, an aesthetic object. To take an example: modern critical theories such as Richard's or, even more so, Barthes's, couldn't care less about biography.[6] That is, they couldn't care less about the individual *chronicle* of an author; they couldn't care less about the historical chronicle of a period. In general, they couldn't care less about history. They're interested in the work.

But what is it in the work that they're interested in? They're interested in what can be called the work's aesthetic structure, in the aesthetic conceived of as a structure. If we ask, for example, where a fellow such as Barthes situates himself: he calls himself a structuralist, of course, but what does he actually concern himself with? He has to do with the work of art as an aesthetic object. He doesn't ask himself: How does it happen that such-and-such a work is considered to be, exists as, an aesthetic object? That is, he doesn't at all ask about the cultural phenomenon of the aesthetic object as such. He simply asks himself about what he calls structures. That is to say that, instead of constructing an aesthetics of a Platonist kind, he defines the [beautiful][7] in itself and so on.

That's very schematic, but, broadly speaking, it comes down to that. He thinks that – here he's an Aristotelian, if you will – he thinks that the beautiful is in the thing itself, that the structure of the beautiful, or the Platonic structure of the beautiful, is inscribed in the thing itself, not outside the thing. The structure is in the work. So reading structures, bringing out the work's structures, is practically a reading of the aesthetic as such: the aesthetic is now no longer an ideology of the transcendence of the beautiful with regard to the work of art. It's a reading of the immanence of the structures of the beautiful, of the aesthetic structures in the work itself.

This is very important, because it's what distinguishes [Barthes] from a structuralism that calls itself structuralism, but is in fact just one of the by-products of the classic aesthetic tradition. I think that that's what Barthes is, to a great extent. There are other things in him, but, finally, that's what it comes down to. That's the side he leans towards, that's where he lands, where he's going to land. On the one hand – although there's another form of structuralism, but one presupposing, precisely, all the questions that all these currents fail to put to the work of art itself.

Optional Visibility: Roland Barthes and Jean-Pierre Richard

Take a fellow like Richard: I'm talking to you about him on the basis of what I know about him. A fellow like Richard also assumes the work of art to be aesthetic. He doesn't ask what allows us to say that it's an aesthetic work. That's the fundamental question.

Richard makes an inventory of the work's themes [*thématique*]. In his way, he studies a certain structure of the work, but not a structure in Barthes's sense: a system of signifiers, each of which is implied by the others, which refer one to the other and so on, forming a closed system, the very opening of which has a prior closure as its condition of possibility. In Richard, it's a question of bringing out themes that it's a question of discovering through variations. The work of art is conceived of as a kind of symphony, which is itself conceived of as the elaboration of a whole series of basic themes that run through the work, both when they're visible and also when they're hidden. It's a question of making them visible. It's a question of making the hidden visible by setting out from that which is visible of the visible.

The whole problem lies there, precisely; for what is the visible? The visible is what is seen. It's hidden, it's interpreted as hidden setting out from what can be seen of it when it's visible. This visible has to be visible for everyone, for Richard himself. That is, setting out from what he sees, he makes a choice in the work, bearing on a selection that he makes in the work of the themes corresponding to his own vision. You know Éluard's phrase: 'reality should not be seen the way I am'.[8] It's a little bit like that. Richard sees Mallarmé the way he, Richard, is. And, setting out from that, he develops a kind of inventory of themes [*thématique*], the emergence of the basic themes, exactly as in a symphony – setting them, if need be, in relation with each other; but there can be several relatively interdependent themes that criss-cross, intersect, play hide-and-seek, go chasing after each other, catch up with each other, fail to catch up with each other. The fact of not catching up is a distance inscribed, in any case, between two existing themes, just as the fact of catching up defines a space.

It's this space of the theme – the space of fluid, flowing, running themes, themes that are parallel, are not parallel, that cross each other, criss-cross each other, are superimposed on each other, hide each other – which makes up the work. This makes for a type of analysis much more subjective than Barthes's analysis. For Barthes brings out the structure of the aesthetic as such, whereas Richard brings out, not the structures of the aesthetic as such, but, as it were, the currents or themes running through the aesthetic as such.

Richard's advantage over Barthes – I'm not talking about an absolute advantage, but about the advantages that Richard, as he sees it, has over Barthes – is that this allows him to remain in the tradition, to remain in the literary tradition, because this will allow him to reintroduce the individual's history, the author's history. The themes are revealed only by setting out from a kind of mélange, in which there intervene both the reading of the themes – that is to say, the observation of their presence in the work, the observation of the visible – and also, more importantly, the fact that Richard sees what he wants to see: he sees himself in the work.

Hence all the themes of sensibility, of sensation – in sum, the sort of literary Epicureanism which forms the ground for his interpretation, which is his own ideology, his own relation to life. It's enough to know him a little to understand that it's a personal affair. It's not an academic work. It's a personal affair, a way not just of living out his relations to the academic world, but of integrating his relations to life and the academic world in a thesis. When one succeeds at that, it's grandiose! That's the ideal of all the people who, because they're academics, want you to think they aren't. When one succeeds at that, one is at least free vis-à-vis academe: one explains to the academic sorts that if one has written this thesis, it wasn't at all to please them, but to please oneself. The best proof is that the demonstration of the thesis is the life one leads day after day. When one's thesis links up with daily life, one is free, one is free vis-à-vis academe.

I said that Richard's advantage over Barthes is that the fact of talking about not a structure of the aesthetic, but the themes that run through the aesthetic field, makes the aesthetic field not a closed world defined by its structure, as in Barthes, but, as it were, the milieu in which the themes manifest themselves. Like some kind of open garden or open field in which you see, all of a sudden, as if in a movie camera's field of view, children who start running every which way through the greenery. Well now, these children come from somewhere. In Barthes's structure, in the closed field, there are no children running around. What is there doesn't come from anywhere. An immobile structure commands all the variations: if things go rusty somewhere, they go rusty because there's no movement. Whereas, in Richard's inventory of themes [*thématique*], if something is running around somewhere, it's because it comes from somewhere; there is something that runs *through*. You have a juxtaposition in the immobile space which is that of the aesthetic field as such, and themes that traverse it and run through it.

Thus you have a dissociation, whereas, in Barthes, you have an immanent theory of the structure in relation to its object, since it's the very structure of the thing. In [Richard], you have themes that appear in the aesthetic as a field that can be traversed by different themes. In Mallarmé, the aesthetic field can be traversed by such-and-such a theme: modesty, frigidity, or whatever one likes ... crystal, inhuman transparency. Or by other themes in the case of others. At any rate, every author has access to the aesthetic field insofar as he's an author, and he sends his favourite personal projections running through it. It's a private projection: there's a screen, everyone has his screen, the aesthetic field, and then he sets his projections to running through it.

The projections, however, come from elsewhere. This allows Richard to synthesize the equivalent of a classic aesthetics, the new presentations of the field of classic aesthetics, [and] the field of biography: that is, history as personal chronicle, individual chronicle. So he fabricates a psychology that jibes with what he wants to demonstrate. Generally speaking, he says that that's how things happen. Given that old Mallarmé has sent this or that theme running through the green prairie of the aesthetic (it's never green, the prairie of the aesthetic, above all not in Mallarmé), but, in any case, he sends it running through it because the aesthetic obviously belongs to him by rights, as is well known. Authors, artists, have free admission: for them, it's always Sunday in the museums.

Whereas it's not that in [Barthes]. It's not always the same characters who stroll through the museums, who enter the museums. There are different ways of strolling through a museum.

The problem that arises for Richard is precisely that of reconciling the old conception of literary history as the chronicle of a life with – what a coincidence! – aesthetic value. And then, on the other hand, with what we can't call, in his case, the structure of the aesthetic as such, but, let us say, movements that traverse, that leave traces, that criss-cross: almost shivers, currents, currents of wind, I wouldn't say currents of air, because it's not ... Yes, in a word, currents that traverse. There's a kind of individual current, it's a kind of circulation.

Intervention: 'Richard ... the theme of fluidity that we discover again, it seems, in flowing water, the water of the stream ...'.

Why, that's fantastic! I didn't know as much about Richard. Because that means he's found a theme that's the very reflection of his own practice. That's absolutely incredible! Because, finally, when we talk about a theme, the presupposition is the idea that such-and-such traverses something, a world in which it has the right to, or in which it can move about freely, and that that confers on it its essence of aesthetic theme. That's the point. At night, all cats are grey. In the aesthetic field, all themes are aesthetic, at bottom. It's something like that.

So, as a result, what characterizes the themes is the fact of traversing – in other words, it's the ability to vary, to change, while simultaneously remaining true to themselves. Unfaithful steadfastness, steadfast infidelity. In short, the themes change: that's what allows them to become invisible, although they're visible in and of themselves. Finally, visibility disappears the moment it is taken up theoretically in the form of a theme, because being visible isn't what makes a theme a theme. What makes a theme a theme isn't its empirical visibility. It's the capacity to be visible or invisible by choice. Thus the inner essence defining the theme as such in that world is the possibility of circulating. A theme circulates, it's fluid.

It's amazing, this business, after all.

A Space of Freedom

This poses two problems. An aesthetics – more precisely, this kind of conception of literary history – obviously poses a whole slew of theoretical problems. The first is the problem of biography, that is, the problem of the type of history. There's a railway car that's hitched to another, but the tracks aren't the same. It's the problem of the Russian border – if only they could circulate with Western cars and Russian cars on the same tracks, but the gauge isn't the same. You can say that the difference in gauge leads to a theoretical discrepancy [*écartèlement*] between the two. And that's what happens, because the theoretical status of biography, of the author's individual psychological biography, has absolutely nothing to do, firstly, with a possible history and secondly, with the world or aesthetic space, precisely, in which all these free movements will occur.

These are themes in freedom; it's the freedom of themes. Finally, this aesthetic world is defined by the freedom of themes – essentially, that is, by freedom, which is an old theme. Not in Richard's sense. It's an old concept which essentially defines the aesthetic world as the realm in which one is free, in which one is at home; it's the theme of the [*bei sich*].[9] In Kant, that's it, more or less, and in Hegel too: the aesthetic is freedom in sensuous immediacy, it's the fact of being able to represent an idea in a body, an individual history, a face or an image.

If, finally, we ask ourselves what constitutes this freedom, if we carry out a structural analysis of the relationship of this aesthetic world 'at home', we observe two things; we observe that the structure of this world implies two things. To begin with, a space in which different circuits unfold, different themes possessing a real individuality. These aren't just any themes. They're themes that excite individuals – individualized themes, which unfold and develop freely. And this liberty of movement with respect to the immobility of the field – because it's a field that's defined as aesthetic, yet has no structure at all – what does it mean?

Very simply, it means that what's involved is a space of freedom. It's the abstract representation of the point of view of an analysis. What theoretical structure do Richard's affirmations imply? It's that there's a space that's the space of the aesthetic as such and that the way of inhabiting this space is the way the themes inhabit it, that is, circulate freely in it. It's freedom of circulation, of imagining oneself physically, in one's relationship to this aesthetic world as a space, by way of the freedom to circulate. You go wherever you like, on condition that you always remain yourself. Wherever you go, you'll always be yourself. That's what freedom is. Become who you are: that is, travel about and you'll always be yourself and you'll fulfil yourself by travelling about. That's freedom of circulation.

Obviously, it's a very particular figuration that clearly expresses the projection of his own desires: the desire to be free everywhere, wherever one may be, whether it's London, Edinburgh, Madrid or wherever. But that's another matter; that's the personal side of the affair. It's

Richard's own freedom of circulation, his wish to be free, to circulate everywhere. ... Whatever country one lives in, one is just as free – in the university too, by the way. The fact that one is free in the university proves that one is free everywhere. It's the proof, the most convincing demonstration, that one might also not have been there. The academic necessarily conceives of the university as a prison, so that if he manages to show that the university is freedom, what's to be said of everything else? Can you imagine? Everything in life becomes easy!

I'm joking. The structure of this relationship, however, is a very special one. An analysis of this kind, which we can make of Richard himself, is already an introduction to what literary history can be. It implies a reflection on the existing work, on a signifying phenomenon that has a socially determined status. To say that Richard wrote his dissertation because he's an academic or to say that so-and-so wrote his work because he's a great writer comes down to the same thing: it's a matter of putting a work's concrete, aesthetic reality, or a work's academic reality and so on, into relation with the social status not of its author, but, if you will, of its production. Or, more exactly, of putting it into relation with the work's social status, which makes it possible to talk about it as such. If we're talking about Richard, it's because he has written a book that everyone is talking about, that everyone has read. This means that he has produced a cultural object. It's not in everyone's power to produce a cultural object. That's the starting point for any possible reflection.

A Pathology of Literary History

That's it: prolegomena to any future reflection on literary history. To try to account, to begin with, for that which no literary historian accounts for: the fact that, if he has the right to try his hand at the difficult task of literary history, it's with respect to existing works that are given to him as his absolute point of departure. They never call that into question.

That's the point on which everything turns. If we begin to call that into question, we send everything flying. That turns everything topsy-turvy. How does it happen that I, Richard, *anno* 1960, can write a book about Mallarmé? Everything's there! Mallarmé is an object of culture, a cultural object. This supposes that Richard hasn't chosen his authors, his author, at all: he has chosen to produce literary criticism of a cultural object that the culture he lives in has designated as a cultural object for him. In other words, the quality 'literary work' isn't at all the product of literary criticism. It's quite simply the object the critic receives from the cultural heritage as such. No one has ever worked differently. No one has ever rescued an author whom no one knew from oblivion without providing the demonstration that he was a great author; but then he is the one who imposes cultural recognition of the work on his times. A fellow who rescues an unknown from oblivion is himself known on condition that – and rescues his unknown author from oblivion only on condition that – he himself is recognized as having effectively rescued from oblivion an unknown who deserved to be known. This means that the instrument of cultural recognition is a fellow who was unknown.

The funny thing about this whole business is that when it doesn't succeed, no one notices. There is never acknowledgement of this sort of failure in history: no one knows all the literary miscarriages the whole world over, no one knows the thousands and tens of thousands of young ladies who, now, write novels every day. Their boyfriends know them and they can render service to their boyfriends. As authors, however, they don't exist. There is no pathology of literary history. That's the funny thing. Or, more exactly, if one poses the problem of a possible pathology of literary history, one sends all classical aesthetics flying, all the unreflected presuppositions of classic literary history.

Because when we ask: What explains the fact that a work of art is known as such, [that it has historical status][10] as such, since history presents it to the person who is going to comment on it? When we ask that, we ask ourselves a question that could be put differently, but it comes to the same thing: What explains the fact that everything written by folks who thought they were writing a decisive work of art has remained a dead letter? It's exactly the same question. The only trouble is that, to be able to ask ourselves that question about them, we would have to have documentation at our disposal, that is, we would have to have at our disposal what has in fact been lost. In general, what's lost historically is lost *tout court*. As a rule, it ended up in our grandmothers' attics and then, one fine day, it was thrown out and went up in smoke. In contrast, we have at our disposal what has been historically preserved, because it has been granted the status of an aesthetic work. We work on what exists, what has been handed down, not on what has been lost.

Note, however, that one could make an attempt at working on what has been lost, because some of the things that were stored in attics exist. Not all attics have gone up in smoke or been sold off at auction.

That would be an extremely interesting counter-demonstration. One could try to elaborate a literary counter-history, a history of literary miscarriage, the history of the non-accession to literary status of works that were nevertheless conceived of as literary by their authors. That would be truly interesting, yet no one has ever tried to do it. That would be an extraordinarily convincing counter-demonstration.

Obviously, a fellow who retrieves minor authors and comments on them ... in any case, however, minor authors are minor authors because they're recognized as such. They have a status; there is a hierarchy in their aesthetic recognition; they're [not nothing].[11] But a fellow who rescues a total unknown from silence and gains recognition for him: firstly, he would have to have the unknown's work at his disposal and secondly, he would have to succeed in gaining recognition for it; that is to say, he would have to bring off, in his way, a literary production which, in its kind and at its level, would correspond, precisely, to what the fellow who wrote the literary work thus rescued from oblivion would have failed to do, or, let us say, would not have succeeded in doing.

If he succeeds, it's for reasons completely unlike the other fellow's: because the cultural world in which this enterprise succeeds is altogether different. Everything starts there.

A History of Non-literature

Paradoxically, that can be developed: one can construct literary history [*faire l'histoire littéraire*]. Constructing literary history implies the possibility of constructing a history of non-literature. Not only works of art that have been completely forgotten by history, or destroyed, but also works that have been received by history as non-literary – all the sub-production that is considered non-literary.

It's the same thing. To construct the history of literature considered as such is the same thing as to construct the history of non-literature, or to construct the history of the pathology ... or to construct, if you like, a history, a pathology, the pathological history of literary pathology. In other words, a history of what has absolutely miscarried as such. A history of what has succeeded, but as non-literary. And a history of what has succeeded, but as literary.

You can see the three degrees. If you want to construct a history of literature, you have to construct a history of what was intended to be literary but miscarried as literary, on the one hand, and you have simultaneously to construct a history of what was produced and has succeeded, but has not received the benediction of literature and isn't considered literary (it can have been intended as literary or intended as non-literary by its authors).

For example, a journalist doesn't have literary pretensions, generally speaking, except when he writes in *Le Figaro* or newspapers of that sort. His pretension is to write newspaper articles. In general, he doesn't assemble them in collected works, except for François Mauriac. (That's another story; it's a pathology that's not a pathology of literary history.)

Thus you have to be able to do three things at once. That is to say that the fellow who takes up literary history with the idea that he can construct literary history all by itself is on the wrong track, because he can construct literary history only on condition that he constructs the three histories just mentioned, or on condition that he reflects on the possibility of constructing those three histories at once in the way he broaches a literary work as such: in the fact that he acknowledges from the start, absolutely and radically, taking it into consideration in what he does later, that if he is discussing a literary work, it's quite simply because it has cultural status and has been consecrated as such by the whole tradition that has handed it down to him and so on, and because he himself is defined, in the prevailing intellectual division of labour and the division of intellectual labour produced by the value judgements existing in the contemporary world, as a function of that work, as occupying the place of a critic vis-à-vis that work.

There haven't always been critics in the division of labour; that's a phenomenon one would have to account for. That is to say that a fellow who undertakes to construct a work's literary history has simultaneously to ask, as his absolute point of departure, what allows him to consider a literary work as literary, when it is in fact acknowledged by history, when it is in fact a cultural phenomenon, on the one hand. On the other, he should ask what allows him to perform his function as a critic. He should ask himself what the fact that he is able to speak about it as a critic represents from the cultural point of view and what it represents in his relationship to the aesthetic object that he will judge and elaborate. He should situate himself as a critic not just with respect to his object, but also in the historical context in which he himself has to situate his object. He should take a historical view both of the situation and of the modality of his object as aesthetic, of course, and of himself as a possible critic of this aesthetic object.

This means that a historian who wants to write the history of literature can't be a historian of literature if he doesn't know what history is and doesn't know what a possible history is in which a historian is himself situated at the very moment he sets out to construct the historical theory of an object bequeathed him by history. Obviously, he has to dispose of a historical theory that allows him to think this paradoxical situation: that of being culturally situated with respect to a cultural object and, at the same time, of being able to produce a discourse that isn't historical about this cultural object that finds itself historically situated, historically confronting him, a critic who has a historically determinate place confronting this object. Or, let us say, a discourse which is historical, but which, in history itself, isn't exposed to the vicissitudes of the historical conjuncture: everything known as relativism and so on, or as historicism.

How is it that one can say something certain, something absolute, theoretically absolute, in a historian's situation [*situation historienne*]? In the situation, that is, of an individual who reflects on a historical result, who tries to construct the theory of it, although he is himself caught up in the history that allowed him to begin making this reflection and, of course, to pursue it?

That's the presupposition implicit in every attempt at literary history.

A Certain Type of History

If we reflect systematically, we [can] define the conditions of possibility of a literary history. Obviously, this presupposes that we first define the conditions of possibility of a history in general. So we come back to the beginning here. What theories allow us to think a history in general? First question. Second question: What theories allow us to think a cultural object that is determinate, that is, transmitted, given, in a historical situation determined as literary and therefore as aesthetic? In other words, we have to think a history that makes it possible not to dissolve the aesthetic specificity of an object that is literary, cultural, poetic, etc. – whatever one likes (broadly, this holds for all aesthetic objects) – in the determinate historical situation through which it is given and by which it is given and handed down.

It is true that Mallarmé exists for us only because he has been handed down to us as such, because he was the object of a historical judgement that has been handed down to us as such. But it's also true that the relationship to Mallarmé isn't a historical relationship. It's a relationship which is experienced in history, but which is experienced as non-historical, because the relationship of a reader of Mallarmé's to Mallarmé is an unmediated, direct relationship that stands in relation to Mallarmé's aesthetic signification, but not at all in relation to history. That isn't experienced that way at all. It's experienced directly.

Hence we need a history that accounts for ... I mean, we need a theory of history that allows us to assume the whole of historical reality, the entire reality of the historical conditions in which a cultural object is given as an object of reflection to a man who has a social function in the social or technical division of intellectual labour and is, on those grounds, a critic. We need a theory which allows us to account for that and which simultaneously allows us to account, through this historical, completely historical, situation, for the direct contact of consumption between a reader of Mallarmé's and Mallarmé.

The fellow who devours Mallarmé doesn't devour the theory of history. Nevertheless, we need a theory of history that allows us to account simultaneously for the historical character of the situation and also for the fact that the critic, like anyone who consumes Mallarmé, has direct contact with Mallarmé and that this contact isn't a historical contact. This presupposes another necessary condition: a theory of history that makes this direct contact possible, that makes possible the existence of a certain level in history through history, a level at which this contact comes about directly through the historical situations themselves.

This presupposes the existence of a certain level that is in some sense unvarying, stable – a certain stability of meanings, representing a certain type of contact that remains relatively constant across the historical variations themselves. It represents the need to think a certain type of history, a certain historical theory that would allow us to think the possibility of a certain level of direct relationship between a reader of Mallarmé's and Mallarmé, whether this direct relationship obtains in 1910 or in 1963, such that the relationship of the reader to Mallarmé in 1910 and the relationship of the reader to Mallarmé in 1963 has, despite all the differences imposed by the historical situation, even on the reader's taste and so on – such that the two have something in common, such that there is something that subsists.

Otherwise, we couldn't talk about Mallarmé. It's not only because he's handed down to us by the historical tradition that we can talk about him. It's because the type of contact that Mallarmé's contemporaries had with him has remained – basically, with variations in the details – the same as the one we have with him now. There's no doubt about it: the reader who reads Mallarmé now and who reads what a reader of Mallarmé's used to read recognizes a contemporary in him, although they aren't contemporaries historically speaking.

There are no other possibilities. There can be variations; there can be historical misunderstandings about a writer. Béranger: it's common knowledge that everyone liked Béranger, Goethe especially,[12] or Flaubert.[13] We can, however, say that history imposes a real test and, ultimately, eliminates contingent variations in that sense. They're not at all contingent in fact, but they're contingent as far as aesthetic judgement goes. If Béranger was so greatly appreciated, it was due to the chauvinism of the French Napoleonic Left: Napoleon was here, he slept in this bed, 'how happy one is in a garret when one is twenty!' and the like.[14] That is to say, a political ideology which thought its nostalgia by way of the Napoleonic myth. That's why Goethe was of the opinion that Béranger was a splendid fellow, because Goethe had, ultimately, preserved a certain nostalgia for Napoleon during Metternich's reaction. Napoleon was, after all, the Civil Code and all the rest of it. Béranger was the same thing, finally, the tricolour and all that – a sort of sentimentality, the

perceived historical element of that kind, the one, that
is, which corresponds to determinate cultural situations.
History itself sorts things out.[15]

In fact, Goethe himself has survived what we can call
the danger of historical misunderstanding that threatens
every writer. But Béranger hasn't. After a certain amount
of time has passed, one can sort things out in pathological
historical situations that disappear with the conditions
that created them; the result is that the historical judgements disappear too, even in apparently literary matters.
Béranger didn't have much to do with literature. But then
the misunderstanding took the following form: people
considered Béranger to be literature. There was quite
simply a wrong address, one address for Béranger in
place of another, Béranger's change of cultural residence.
Everybody thought he lived on the first floor, when he
actually lived in a basement. In fact, it was quite simply
a districting error, a wrong address: the postman made a
mistake.

We need, then, a theory of history that would make it
possible to account for a certain constancy and a certain
stability in the aesthetic contact of a reader who is an
author's contemporary, on the one hand, and a reader's
aesthetic contact with the same author's works in a period
at a great remove from this first contact. The contact of
a contemporary of Racine's is one thing, the contact that
today's reader has to him is quite another, yet they have
something in common. Not at all in the sense of an anthropology, that's not it at all; still, we have to account for this.
The fact that they have something in common is a possible
historical phenomenon and we have to account for it.

Thus we need a history that accounts for the possibility
of this relative permanence. There we have the formal
conditions.

This problem must be solved. I could provide some
suggestions on this, but it may be a little too personal.

Obviously, I'd be inclined to resolve this in the following
context. I think that it's on the basis of Marxist theory
alone that we can account for this, because it's the
only theory capable of accounting for all these things

simultaneously – of accounting simultaneously for a given cultural object's historical reality, on the one hand, and the historical situation of the literary critic who sets out to construct a literary history: in other words, to construct the history of this cultural object while also maintaining the possibility of direct aesthetic contact with it.

If you will: when in classic literary history one had to do, as we saw a moment ago, with the dissociation between history as chronicle on the one hand and, on the other, with the aesthetic as such, which detached itself from that chronicle, it was a necessary extension, because it was intended to make up for a lack, because history as such is the reduction of everything that's specifically aesthetic. So what was lacking had to be added. An aesthetic supplement was required, because there was no longer anything aesthetic at all! We have seen that; that is, the inability of all the themes to think their own cohabitation and, at the same time, the need for each of the themes or each of the fundamental concepts to be completed by the concept it lacked, setting out from its own position. It's a bit like the old story that goes 'it's a pity the cities weren't built in the countryside, the air is so pure there'.[16] In the countryside, a fellow misses everything the city offers him, but when he's in the city, he misses everything the countryside would offer him.

Trying to have the city in the country is a bit like the programme of classic literary history, which wants to do history and aesthetics at the same time. The territory is superimposed, because it is, properly speaking, impossible for literary history to have the city in the country.

On a hypothesis like the one I would like to propose – I believe it's the sole hypothesis that meets all the basic prerequisites we've discussed: namely, to account for the cultural character, the cultural and therefore historical status of an object of aesthetic reflection. That is, if you talk about Mallarmé today, the fact is that it's because history gives him to you as a consecrated aesthetic object. That's the first thing.

Secondly: to account for the historical status of the person who talks about that object. If Richard talks about

Mallarmé today, if he has the right to talk about him as a literary critic, it's because there has existed in contemporary society, for quite some time now, a social function in the intellectual division of labour known as Literary Criticism, known as the academics or non-academics, who have the function, or assign themselves the function, of producing literary history in general, because they feel a need for it. Here, we could ask ourselves why they feel a need for it. (That's another matter. Because there are entire civilizations that get along without critics or historians of literature, or even without any history at all, civilizations that experience their history without reflecting on it.) Thus we need a historical theory that simultaneously accounts for this last phenomenon, that is, the possibility of a direct contact between today's reader and Mallarmé – between Richard and Mallarmé – which has something in common with the direct contact that a contemporary of Mallarmé's had with Mallarmé's works.

Thus we need a theory of history which in itself implies, simultaneously, the cultural status of the aesthetic object, on the one hand, and the historical status of the critic and the profession of critic, that is, history's relationship to the historian, which is fundamental. On the other hand, the possibility of a direct relationship – let us say, a relationship of aesthetic judgement broadly speaking, of aesthetic consumption – between the aesthetic object in question and any possible reader, between Mallarmé and all his possible readers. If we want to call things by their names, a certain permanence, a certain constancy of what Hegel would call the sphere of the aesthetic, which, however, is precisely not a sphere, because it isn't round at all: the aesthetic *stratum*, the aesthetic *level*.

A Non-historical Relation to Historical Objects

This level concerns what is called, in Marxist theory, the level of aesthetic ideology – of art as ideology. Obviously, that's a very general, very abstract expression; yet there are, in Marx, all the basics required to construct a theory of art as ideology in that sense: in other words, as a stratum of activity that at once produces and consumes aesthetic objects, thought [*réfléchi*] in the form of aesthetic creation, aesthetic judgement, taste and so on, everything that belongs to a relatively stable stratum possessing a history, of which it is possible to construct a history.

There we have the paradox, because, if it is in fact possible to construct a history of aesthetic objects as such, a history of the aesthetic stratum as such – finally, that's what it comes down to – the hypothesis of a Marxist history implies the hypothesis that it is possible to construct a history of strata comprising the ideological strata or the different ideological levels or different ideological objects, each of which presupposes the possibility of a history that is based, fundamentally, on general history, yet is a specific history.

Practically speaking, what does that mean? It means that we have to do, in the case of Marxist theory, with a theory that implies the possibility of all existing ideological forms. We can construct a history of philosophy, we can construct a history of morals, we can construct a history of religion, we can construct a history of art, we can construct a history of aesthetic judgement, we can construct a history of the beautiful and so on. Thus we can construct a history of literature as aesthetic object, because the possibility of it is founded, theoretically founded, in the very conception of history.

That's why I say that this seems to me to be the only possible hypothesis. It supposes all kinds of explanations and developments to justify it. It is there that, at least as far as I'm concerned, I can make out the possibility of posing, in an existing theory, all the problems we encounter in this connection as soon as we ask what's involved when a fellow sits down to write about an author who has produced a work that is called literary. Ultimately, it's simply a matter of accounting theoretically for what he is doing, nothing else!

The fellow who sets about writing about Rousseau is doing something. What happens? He has to do with an object. What is this object? He is a fellow writing about

Rousseau in 1963. What is this function of writing about Rousseau? And he writes about Rousseau in the belief that Rousseau is a literary object, an aesthetic object. After all, he can consider him to be another object; he can consider Rousseau to be a political thinker or what have you. The historian of literature who talks about Rousseau as a literary creator, however, considers him to be an aesthetic object, a literary object. So that has to be accounted for, because it's true, there's no denying it. It has to be accounted for, however, in a theory that makes it possible to think, simultaneously, the historical conditions of possibility of this typical relationship, of this historically determined relationship that is the relationship of a literary critic to a work which has been historically registered and consecrated as aesthetic, without supposing that the fellow who's going to construct the history of literature will be conflated with the fellow who's going to construct the history of the development of societies. The one bears no relation to the other, or rather, no immediate relation to the other.

Obviously, all this is based on the history of societies, that goes without saying. Through this history of societies, however, a certain type of non-historical relationship is envisaged. That's the paradox. We have to construct a theory of history that accounts for the possibility of a non-historical relationship to historical objects themselves. That's it, ultimately; that's what I would say.

That is why I give this answer: the only theory, to my knowledge, which makes it possible to construct a theory of a non-historical relationship to an aesthetic object or an ideological object in general, yet which is at the same time a historical theory, that is, a historical theory allowing for the possibility of a non-historical relationship to historical objects, is Marxism. It's Marx's theory. Marx didn't explain all that, but he contains everything required to explain it.

What do you think?

Intervention: '[What I'm asking you for] here is personal advice – I'd like you to tell me where in Marx and in what way?'

I can't tell you where or in what way. In what way, yes, but as for 'where'? There is no 'where'. What we find when we look at editions of texts by Marx or Marxists on aesthetics doesn't have much to do with these problems. Generally, they're texts containing aesthetic judgements pronounced by Marx on this or that author. That's another matter, judging whether a fellow is a powerful sort or a feeble sort. It isn't the beginning of the beginning of literature. It's gastronomy. A fellow is having a bite and he says: 'This beef stew is damned good!' That's all; it's a judgement of taste. You might say that taste is to biochemistry what the judgement of a patron of Pauline's is to literary history. They're of the same general order. You won't find these things in those texts. They're found elsewhere. But you won't find them localized, absolutely not. There isn't a theory of the possibility of the aesthetic anywhere.

We do have a theory, however. We can find in Marx's theory of history, precisely, concepts and the problematic that allow us to answer concrete questions that anyone engaged in constructing literary history or setting out to construct it has to ask himself from the moment he asks: What am I in the process of doing? And what gives me, on any grounds whatever – historical, theoretical and so on – the right to do what I'm doing? Because I have every right to do it, there's no problem there. If one does literary history, one doesn't for a single second question the fact that one has a right to. This right which, like all rights, isn't called into question – yet it isn't at all natural for a fellow who would contest it, say, or for a civilization in which it wouldn't be considered natural (that is to say, for other forms of historical existence).

So this right that seems so natural *is* called into question. It's therefore revoked[17] as natural by historical consciousness, even the most elementary historical consciousness. This elementary historical consciousness is there in Montaigne himself.[18] The savages and all that, the Pyrenees that you-know-who is supposed to have made into one of the proofs of the existence of God. A mountain isn't bad as proof of the existence of God. Geography comes in handy for everything, but it's absolutely elementary that that's not where this has its place. Yet it raises a question, at any rate.

It raises a question: What gives you the right to consider it natural to do what you're doing? It calls into question the natural character of the act by which a fellow enters into a relation to an aesthetic work in order to construct its literary history. It calls its natural character into question; that is, it calls its historical character into question and brings it out. [But] we have by no means resolved the problem if we leave it at that: we lapse into historical relativism. At that point, one says: that's how it is because that's how it is now and that's all there is to it; earlier, it was different. All apologists and all travellers admire that sort of thing.

There exists a sort of theoretical tourism of this kind, which makes people love it when they find at home what they don't find elsewhere and the other way around. The watchword of all of them is: 'one can never venture far enough in search of the pleasure of coming back home',[19] because tourism is a way of travelling around in order to realize that, finally, one is right not to leave. Thus there are people who don't go to the bother of travelling because they know ahead of time that they'll be better off at home when they come back. So they don't leave the house. Not leaving home gives you all the historians of literature. Rather than going and having a look around in the countries where there's no literary history, they stay home, because they know that they'll be coming back home in any case! If you want to go back home, I've got a good address for you – yours! Since they'll be going back home, they prefer not to leave, so they engage in tourism where they are, by proxy and provisionally. They put possible tourism in brackets and then they say to themselves: 'No problem at all, because the fact is that if I go have a look next door, I'll be coming back home in any case. So let us ply our trade, let us cultivate our gardens!'

Beyond Foucault

Intervention: 'To imitate Foucault's way of doing things,

in some sense. He constructs a history of reason, not of madness.[20] To construct a history of literature by constructing a history of non-literature. That goes back to what you were saying a little while ago.'

Ah, yes. Yes, that's it, exactly. There is something in Foucault's way of proceeding that, from the methodological standpoint, goes extraordinarily far beyond his book, which is already extraordinary. There is a phenomenal lesson about methodology there. In Foucault's case, the following happens: Foucault has constructed the history of reason by way of the history of madness. In other words, he has constructed the history of the couple reason/madness. He has shown that this couple was a real couple in the period he studies. We can, however, ask whether this couple wasn't a historically conditioned couple; in other words, whether he hasn't chosen, precisely, a historical period in which this couple existed. For there can be other couples: reason isn't necessarily situated with respect to madness, non-reason isn't necessarily madness. We can even ask whether, even in the seventeenth century, in all the historical periods that Foucault studies, it was madness which was really discriminating in a significant way, as Chapouthier would have put it (he always gave discriminating translation assignments).

The question is whether it's madness that is discriminating: whether, in non-reason, madness holds the dominant place. Foucault doesn't say it's the only place, of course; he knows very well that there are forms of non-reason other than madness. What's more, he says so. But he says that, in the seventeenth century, it was in fact madness that filled the place of non-reason or was, at any rate, the guiding concept in non-reason. If one wants to penetrate non-reason in the seventeenth century, one has to take madness as one's guide.

That's what he says and that's all. He doesn't say that that's all there is. This is a factual question. Not just factual, of course; there are no absolute facts. But we need to find out whether that works in every case in order to say whether one really has to broach non-reason by way of madness. This question is much too big. We can talk about it.

Methodologically, I find the Fouks's extraordinary book very convincing, but I have questions, historical questions, about certain points in it, because I'm not sure that there's only madness – rather, that madness is always the privileged means of access, the occupant *par excellence* of the place of non-reason. I think there are other access routes to non-reason. I wonder whether we shouldn't try out other ways of penetrating non-reason, that is to say, whether we shouldn't take other concepts as guides. More exactly, since it's not a question of concepts, since these are realities searching for their concept that don't manage to find it – I wonder whether we shouldn't take something other than madness as our guide, to see what the result might be. To see whether we wouldn't discover other things that might allow us to verify the Fouks's hypothesis, namely, that it is indeed by way of madness that we should penetrate non-reason, because madness alone holds the keys to this world.

Supplementary Note on History
(undated: 1965–1966?)

1. It should be perfectly clear that, in everything that has been said about history, what is at issue is a search for the definition of the concept of the *historical*, that is, for the specific object of a theory of history.[1] When it was said that the time of history is not the empty ideological time *in which* historical events unfold, but the specific time of the mode of production under consideration, of the determinate mode of production in question, it is clear that what is envisaged is solely that time which can be called *historical*.

That, of course, implies a distinction which, as we shall see, is an integral part of the proposed definition of history and historical time, a discriminating distinction which, among all events and facts, all phenomena with the power to affect the existence of the people living in a given mode of production, distinguishes those which deserve to be singled out as historical to the exclusion of the others. In other words, we no more consider all events or phenomena of the human existence of a given society to be historical than we consider the first time that comes along to be historical, whether it is biological, physical, psychological, or of some other kind. On the other hand, and as a function of this pertinent distinction, we cannot make the claim that everything that happens in the existence of human beings, who always live in a social formation that comes under a determinate mode of production, belongs to history, and that the theory of history can therefore claim to provide theoretical knowledge of everything appertaining to this human existence.

If history wishes to respect the concept of its object, it must restrict its claims to establishing the intelligibility of its object, to the exclusion of all the phenomena that do not come under its concept. This does not mean that such-and-such a discipline, which *does* take these non-historical phenomena as its object, need not consider historical reality, as though it were purely and simply without effect on the object of that discipline. But then history appertains to this new object, if at all, solely as one of its conditions, not as its essence or even its dominant condition. The same necessity which requires us to give a discriminating definition of the historical as such also dictates that the theory of history restrict its reign to the limits of its object so defined, leaving to other disciplines the knowledge of the non-historical, which is distinguished from the historical by the definition of the specificity of the historical itself.

2. What has been said about history so far implies, obviously, that we have to provide this definition of the historical. To date, we have only envisaged history in the form of *historical temporality* and have shown that this historical temporality was conceivable only as the process of existence specific to each mode of production. Thus the object of the theory of history is the history or process of existence (and development or non-development) of the different modes of production. It is by relating all theoretical problems to its object that history can define the specificity of its object, in the different forms of its existence and apprehension.

On Genesis (1966)

I would like to make one point more precise, one that is no doubt not very clear in my letter.[1]

In the schema of the 'theory of the encounter' or theory of the 'conjunction', intended to replace the ideological (religious) category of genesis, there is room for what we may call *linear genealogies*.

Thus, to return to the example of the logic of the constitution of the capitalist mode of production in *Capital*:

1. The elements defined by Marx 'combine'. I prefer to say (in order to translate the term *Verbindung*) that they 'conjoin' by 'taking hold' in a new structure. This structure cannot be thought, in its irruption, as the effect of a filiation; it must be thought as the effect of a *conjunction*. This new Logic has nothing to do with the linear causality of filiation or with Hegelian 'dialectical' causality, which merely says out loud what is implicit in the logic of linear causality.

2. Yet *each* of the elements that come together and combine in the conjunction of the new structure (in the case to hand, accumulated money-capital; 'free' labour-power, that is, labour-power divested of its work tools; and technological inventions) is itself, as such, a *product*, an *effect*.

What is important in Marx's demonstration is that the three elements are not *contemporaneous* products of one and the same situation. In other words, it is not the feudal mode of production which, by itself, thanks to a providential finality, simultaneously engenders *the three elements* required for the new structure to 'take hold'. Each of these elements has its own 'history' or *genealogy* (to borrow a concept of Nietzsche's that Balibar has used felicitously in this connection): the three genealogies are relatively *independent*. We even see Marx show that the same element ('free' labour-power) can be produced as the result of *completely different genealogies.*[2]

Thus the genealogies of the three elements are independent of each other, and independent (in their co-existence and the co-existence of their respective results) of the existing structure (the feudal mode of production). This excludes all possibility of a resurgence of the myth of genesis: the feudal mode of production is not the 'father' of the capitalist mode of production in the sense that the latter is contained '*as a seed*' in the first.

3. That said, it remains to conceive the types of causality that might, with respect to these elements (and, generally, with respect to the *genealogy of any element*), intervene in order to account for the *production of these elements* as elements entering into a conjunction that is going to 'take hold' in a new structure.

We must, it seems to me, distinguish here between *two* distinct *types* of causality:

a. *Structural causality*: an element can be produced as a *structural effect*. Structural causality is the *ultimate causality* of every effect.

What does the concept of structural causality mean? It signifies (in very rough terms) that an *effect B* (considered as an element) is not the effect of a *cause A* (another element), but is, rather, the effect of element A insofar as *this element A is inserted into relations* that constitute the *structure* in which A is 'caught up' [*pris*] and situated. Put simply, this means that to understand the production of effect B, it is not enough to consider cause A (immediately preceding, or visibly related to effect B) in isolation, but, rather, cause A as an element of a structure in which it takes its place, hence as subject to the relations, the specific structural relations, that define the structure in question.

A very basic form of structural causality appears, for example, in modern physics when it uses the concept of a *field* and puts into play what may be called the *causality of a field*. In the case of the science of societies, if we follow Marx's thought, we cannot understand such-and-such an economic effect by setting it in relation to an isolated cause; we must set it in relation to the *structure* of the economic (defined by the articulation of the productive forces and relations of production). In the same way, presumably, in psychoanalysis, a given effect (a symptom) is intelligible only as an effect of the *structure of the unconscious*. It is not a given event or element A which produces a given element B, but the defined *structure* of the subject's unconscious which produces effect B.

   b. This law seems to be general. But structural causality defines as structural, hence as a structural effect, *rigorously defined and delimited zones* or *sequences* in which structural causality is realized *in the form of linear causality*. This is what happens, for example, in the *labour process*. Linear mechanical causality (even if it takes complex forms, as it does in machines, these forms remain *mechanical*, that is, linear, *even in feedback* and other cybernetic effects) operates in autonomous, exclusive fashion in a *defined field*, that of the *production of products* in the labour process. To drive in a nail, you hit it with a hammer; to plough up a field, you bring forces to bear on a ploughshare that acts on the earth and so on. This linear-mechanical causality (that which Sartre calls 'analytical reason' ... but beware: what Sartre calls dialectical reason is, despite what he says, just a complex form of analytical reason, just analytical reason)[3] acts this way in producing the same effects by *repetition* and *accumulation*. We see this in Hegel when he discusses quantitative accumulation or the logic of the understanding. Hegel tried to think properly structural effects in the form of a 'qualitative leap'; that is, he tried to shift from linear to structural causality by generating the second from the first (that is why his 'dialectic' is held fast in the empirical categories of the mechanical and linear understanding, despite his *declaration* that they have been surpassed, the concept of 'surpassing' – *Aufhebung* – being the concept that, despite itself, confesses and recognizes this captivity).

Thus there are whole sequences – always defined, however, within *rigorous limits* laid down by structural causality – which are subject to the autonomous play of analytical or *linear causality* (or transitive causality). This appears quite clearly in certain sequences of economic, political and ideological phenomena. This must also appear in psychoanalysis (for example, in certain sequences belonging to the secondary processes. It seems to me that what are called 'secondary formations', such as defensive complexes [*formations défensives*], are examples).

In the case of our three elements, the accumulation of money-capital is ascribable to this mechanism, as are certain sequences that produce the other elements.

In all these cases, however, the limits and 'play' of mechanical causality, as well as the *type of object* it produces, are determined in the last instance by structural causality. We may even go further and say that (mechanical) effects of accumulation can be observed between structural effects (as Marx says: the existence of 'free labour-power' is the result of *several* different, independent processes, whose effects are *added to* each other and reinforced thereby), but that these effects, between which the play of a mechanical causality comes about, are, taken in isolation, structural effects.

I won't develop this any further. I just wanted to point out the principle of this double causality and its articulation, where structural causality determines linear causality.

22 September 1966

How Can Something Substantial Change? (1970)

The question: How can something substantial change in the Party?

The answer of the different groupings, classic groupings or products of May: thanks to the movement of the masses, hence thanks to revolutionary protest by the rank-and-file. But the question: The result has to be an organization, both to harvest the fruit of the masses' protest and to develop this protest! The answer: Let us found a new party or an organization that will disappear, when the time comes, in the new party it will have helped to found. These organizations are today founded on either Trotskyist or Maoist theoretical bases or on traditional petty-bourgeois bases, with multiple variants.

The result: The Party continues to exist. It pursues its traditional political line without being seriously disturbed by these organizations: the small groups irritate it but do not undermine its sense of security. In its fashion, this serenity expresses something concrete.

The question becomes: Can something substantial be changed in the Party *from inside* the Party? Thanks to heightened rank-and-file consciousness that modifies the Party's politics? Thanks to an overt crisis in the Party, thanks to rank-and-file protest, precipitating changes at the top?

This is, obviously, a question of judgement, but I do not believe in a possibility of this sort under present circumstances. It is enough to see how the Party succeeded in 'digesting' the May events, integrating them into its traditional line – to observe how, in particular, it succeeded in treating the student movement – in order to understand that it is quite capable of *absorbing the shock* of even a very big mass movement and maintaining leadership of it. The current political line, which consists in putting the CGT[1] in the forefront and continuing to exist in its shadow, this adroit, effective division of labour, proves that the Party has a broad margin of manoeuvre in which arrangements that stymie action ensure it a maximum of security.

If nothing substantial can be changed in the Party as a result of the action of small groups or oppositional groups, any more than by a possible contradiction between the rank-and-file (of the Party, or even the masses) and the Party leadership, what hope is there?

How will it ever be possible for a change to come about?

To envisage this question in its concrete reality, we have to set out from what was just said (that which is excluded) and, simultaneously, what is presupposed by what was just said: the solidity, the *strength of the Party*, and the Party's resources. The Party will not be changed from outside; it can only be changed from inside. At the same time, however, we just saw that it was not possible to change its inside [*son dedans*]. ... Is there no way out, then?

There remains one way out. It is that the Party is affected (changed) *in its inside by an outside event*, but an event such that it affects it in its inside, in its substance, *political line* and political references.

What might this event be? The answer is simple: an event that very seriously calls into question the political line of reference for the Party, namely, *the political line and the existence of the USSR*. For example, a very serious crisis in the USSR, or a very serious, irremediable crisis of the USSR's international-internationalist politics (a conflict with the USA or China and so on). A very serious crisis of the USSR's political line: this could be a very grave economic-political crisis in the USSR leading to consequences on the order of nationalist disintegration and so on. Something that is hard to imagine and predict.

We have one indication: undeniably, the Czech crisis seriously unsettled, for a time, the Party's line and leadership. By itself, this crisis was able to produce a result that May had failed to: sowing dissension in the Party leadership. This breach was plugged. It is conceivable that more serious events could have more far-reaching consequences in the French Party. However, for as long as its leadership is not divided by the event, by an event capable of dividing it, it will manage to pull its chestnuts out of the fire.

A very grave event calling the references and principles of its political line into question could touch off a grave political crisis thanks to which an opposition could express itself *in the Party itself*, an opposition it would not be possible to overcome with the methods that served for May and the student movement.

One cannot, setting out from there, play the prophet. One can, however, imagine that the masses outside the Party will have their say over a shorter or longer period, including some of the elements organized in oppositional groups. The big question then will be whether the way out of the crisis thus initiated leads left or right. It is likely that Party unity would not survive such a crisis and that the right and the left would regroup in opposed organizations.

28 April 1970

To Gretzky (1973) (extract)

Question: What do you mean by 'historicism'?

Historicism is a form, a relatively modern form, of an old philosophical tradition: temporal *relativism*. It may also, and at the same time, be regarded as the form *empiricism* takes in the field of the knowledge of history.

As relativism's heir, historicism has Heraclitus as its remote ancestor: 'everything flows, one never bathes in the same river twice' and so on.[1] As empiricism's heir, historicism has as its ancestor a good part of eighteenth-century philosophy (Hume, Helvétius and so on) as well as certain aspects of Hegel's philosophy of history.

Closer to our own day, historicism took clear-cut form in the late nineteenth and early twentieth centuries, as a form of the bourgeois philosophy of history, a relativistic-subjectivist-empiricist form made to combat the Marxist theory of history (cf. *Geschichtsphilosophie*, *Geistesphilosophie*, Dilthey, Simmel, Rickert, Mannheim and, of course, Weber – in Italy, Croce and others and in France, more recently, Raymond Aron).[2]

One of the 'ticklish points' in the confrontation between historicism (inherited from Croce, in this case) and Marxism was played out in *Gramsci*, as he tried to 'assume' and 'surpass' Croce's historicism by taking it to the absolute: 'Marxism is the *absolute* historicism.'[3] An interesting (but at the same time a failed) attempt that recalls Lenin's distinction between absolute and relative truth.[4] Gramsci *was looking for* something like what Lenin *found*: Gramsci too 'worked' on the 'relative' (historical = relative), but he believed that he could extricate himself from it by generalizing-absolutizing the relative and relativism – without distinguishing, as Lenin does, the relative from the absolute. But when one tries to *get out* of relativism (historicism) by absolutizing relativism (= absolute historicism), one does not get out of relativism: one remains in it. Lenin's thesis on the distinction between absolute truth and relative truth is one proof ('conscious of itself') of the distance that Marxism takes from historicism (= relativism in history).

Thus historicism is essentially a philosophical position which represents relativism in the domain of knowledge of history.

Its theses are simple.

First thesis. All that exists (whatever the nature of the 'thing' considered may be, whether it is human individuals, institutions, or even mere 'nature', says *The German Ideology*, because nature is always 'transformed by human labour' – example: fruit trees) is historical, including, therefore, knowledge, science and so on.[5]

Second thesis. What does 'historical' mean? Something is historical if it is endowed with an existence *relative* to time, to circumstances that are themselves *temporal* and so on, in the unbroken, perpetually *changing* succession of times and temporal circumstances. An *absolutely* relative existence is historical, hence *completely reducible* to time and temporal circumstances, with no residue that goes beyond [*dépasse*] time and temporal circumstances, whatever the nature of that residue might be.

Third thesis. If everything is historical, knowledge itself is *historical* (in the sense of Thesis 2). In particular, *the knowledge of history is historical*, hence relative to the time and the temporal circumstances of its existence. Thus we have relativism: the knowledge of 'history' belongs (without residue) to the history of which it is the knowledge. In this relativist 'circle', we recognize the empiricist 'circle' too, since knowledge of the object history *is part* of the object 'history'.

Of course, since absolute relativism is untenable (for, at the limit, we cannot even *state* it, as Plato objected),[6] no author (no philosopher or historian) has ever upheld *absolute* relativist-historicist positions. No one has ever maintained (as in the absolute relativistic subjectivism of a Protagoras) that history was just a succession of pure *instants*: it was granted that there are 'periods', 'times', 'epochs', in short, *temporary permanencies* in the general transformation of the course of history. Thus some could maintain that a theory of history (whether a philosophy of history or Marx's theory) were [*sic*] not just the '*expression*' of their time, but that they were *nothing but* the expression of their time and the expression of their time *alone*. This is a way of subordinating and reducing them to the *contingency* of their own historical 'epoch', while contesting any claim they might make to explaining a later 'epoch'. This is how Marx is treated by most bourgeois philosophers of contemporary history. They (Raymond Aron, for example) are very happy to say that Marx 'expressed' a certain number of principles which *expressed* a 'truth' valid for nineteenth-century capitalism; now, however, capitalism has changed![7] One has to recognize Marx's limits: they are the limits of his time. He has to be buried in his own time, to which he belongs: Marx was unable to 'leap out of his own time' (this is what Hegel's particular kind of historicism had already said about philosophy). This philosophical operation is clear: the principle of historicism serves to get rid of Marx, that is, of the scientific principles of the knowledge of history: not only the history of Marx's time, but also (on condition that we 'develop' those principles) our own – and history before Marx as well.

If Marxism well and truly provides scientific principles for the knowledge of history, it cannot be a historicism, that is to say, a philosophical relativism in the field of the knowledge of history – something that would deny it all scientific and, therefore, objective value, and therefore all value *theoretically* independent of time and temporal circumstances. In my essays, I cited Spinoza – the concept of a dog does not bark (= the concept of a dog is not 'canine', is not a dog) – and added that the knowledge of sugar is not sweet, the knowledge of history is not historical (= the theoretical concepts that make knowledge of history possible are not subject to historical relativism).[8]

This does not mean, obviously, that Marxist theory is exempt from the laws that command the historical emergence of scientific theories or that it has existed for all eternity! It does not mean that it has no *history* (every theory, every science has a history). However, the laws *of* history (the history of social formations and also of theories) are precisely not 'historical' laws, that is, relativist-subjectivist laws; they are not 'historicist' laws; they are objective laws and thus non-subjectivist, non-historicist laws.

Historicist relativism in history is therefore (this follows from the preceding distinction) bound up with a certain conception, a certain representation of History: the one we described by saying 1. that everything is historical and 2. that 'historical' designates the fact that every existence is relative to a time and to temporal conditions which are perpetually changing. These characteristics constitute a representation of the 'nature' of history which is *completely different* from the representation corresponding to the scientific concepts of the Marxist theory of history. We may say that, for Marxist theory, the 'object-of-knowledge' (a theoretical object, defined by the system of theoretical concepts) of history has practically nothing to do with the 'object'-History of the historicist representation of History. The historicist representation of history corresponds to an *ideology* of history which systematizes 'self-evident truths' of 'common sense' of the sort: 'everything disappears, everything changes'; truth on this side of the Pyrenees, error on the other side;[9] to each his truth, to each epoch its truth. Historicist ideology takes a (more or less developed) system of these everyday 'self-evident truths' for the *reality* of history. Historicist ideology does not for a single second question the self-evident truths that serve as its justification. If it questioned them, it wouldn't be an ideology.

The *reality* of history, however, is intelligible only on condition that we carry out a theoretical labour (a

change in 'point of view', abandonment of relativist-
subjectivist ideology) culminating in the critique of all
relativist-subjectivist themes, their abandonment and the
production of a system of basic theoretical concepts to
which there corresponds a very different *reality* of history:
history as a process of the emergence, constitution (and
disappearance) of social formations in which modes of
production are 'realized'; the unity of the relations of
production and the productive forces, a history 'driven'
by the struggle of the classes. Historical *time* is thus no
longer the pure succession of changes or the universal
relativism of the *hic et nunc*; it is the time *of* each mode of
production, of the cycles of production and reproduction
and so on. In short, a time to which there correspond
concepts completely different from those of historicist
ideology – let us say, an idea of time to which there
corresponds a completely different 'object' than historicist
ideology's 'object-time'.

There you have, in outline, the theoretical reasons for
which Marxism is not a historicism. That it is called anti-
historicist has to do with the ideological conjuncture in
which it must struggle *against* its historicist interpretation
in order to be itself. Considering it for itself, however, we
would have to say that Marxism *is not* a historicism, or
that it is an a-historicism.[10]

20 January 1973

Draft of a Reply to Pierre Vilar
(undated: 1972? 1973?)

I obviously ran big risks in venturing into the field of history – not the philosophical category of history, but the practitioner's history, the historian's history. And Vilar did very well to point out the hastiness of some of my judgements.[1] I do not think, however, after reading the critique that he was kind enough to devote to me, that he has contested the principle informing them.

For I think that Marxist philosophy's claim to have its say about the work of the historians is in principle well-founded. The first reason is quite simple: it is that there exists in history, as in every science, an ideology of its practitioners, which I have called, after Lenin, their spontaneous philosophy.[2] This spontaneous philosophy, which seems at first sight to be limited to the narrow circle of the relationship between the practitioner and his practice, in fact always harks back to philosophical themes developed outside this practice by the major antagonistic philosophies, let us say, the dominant philosophies and those that contest their domination. While demonstrating this in detail would call for precise investigations, one clearly senses that the Annales School in France, to cite just this grand example, sprang from a political and ideological reaction against the dominant, reactionary academic philosophy, and that behind this reaction lay the reality of the big political struggles that, in France, were to culminate in the Popular Front. There is, however, another reason, which comes under the first: it is that historical science cannot dispense with philosophy, spontaneous or reflected, any more than any other science can. In principle, therefore, philosophy may have its say about the works of the historians. And when the philosophy in question is sustained by the Marxist theory of history, it is entitled to have its say twice over: philosophically and theoretically.

I think it is necessary to clear up a misunderstanding about historicism here, at the outset. When one says, as I have, that Marxism is not a historicism, one is in danger of being misunderstood by the historians, who, not just for semantic reasons but, perhaps, for theoretical reasons as well, believe that history is being called into question, if not indicted.

Let us say, for the sake of brevity, that one may be inclined to think that if Marxism is an anti-historicism, it can only turn away from history or treat history only by reducing it to abstract structures incapable of accounting for historical development, historical struggles and so on. In fact, the very opposite is true, but on *one* condition, which the thesis that Marxism is an anti-historicism is intended, precisely, to bring out. What is this condition? It is the distinction between lived history and the knowledge of history, the distinction between the ideological representations of history and the scientific categories and analyses that lead to the knowledge of history. Marx repeatedly articulated this distinction with a bon mot: if the essence (or knowledge) came down to the phenomenon (to what is immediately given), there would be no need for science (an amusing bon mot that is no doubt inspired by the British one-liner: if my aunt had two wheels ...).[3] Marx articulated the same distinction by saying that it isn't by adding different series together than one succeeds in explaining the functioning of the social whole; or, again, by insisting on the fact that the order of succession of the categories in the realm of theory is not identical with their order of succession in history and so on.[4] Theoretical anti-historicism[5] thus means that the concepts providing the knowledge of history do not exist in an unmediated state in visible history and, more generally, that the knowledge of history, while it too is an event in history, is not historical in the vulgar sense of the term, is not, that is, subjective or relative.

A misunderstanding, I said; but I must add, in view of his criticisms, that there has never been the least misunderstanding between Pierre Vilar and me. Vilar's critiques and reservations are fertile, because they bear on completely different questions, questions internal to an understanding of the logic of the concepts of the Marxist science of history.

Book on Imperialism
(1973) (extracts)

[To my readers]

This book is about a question 'classic' in Marxism since Lenin: imperialism.

Why this book?

For a simple reason. We are living in the 'stage' of imperialism, which is the last stage in the history, that is, the existence, of capitalism. Even if we are struggling against imperialism alongside the working class, we are subject to imperialism. To defeat imperialism, we have to know imperialism; we have to know what distinguishes it from the other stages of capitalism; we have to have as precise an idea as possible of its specific characteristics and mechanisms. It is on this condition alone that the proletarian class struggle will be well conducted and can culminate in revolution, the dictatorship of the proletariat and the construction of socialism on the Long March that will bring us from capitalism to communism.

But, it will be said, these things are well known. Under those conditions, why this book?

These things are well known. ... Is that so very certain? True, we *talk* about imperialism and happily repeat Lenin's formulas about imperialist wars and acts of aggression, about the dividing up of the world, about the pillaging of the non-imperialist countries' riches and so on. True, we supported the heroic struggle of Indochina's peoples against French imperialism and then American imperialism, both of which were militarily and politically defeated on the ground by an adversary smaller than they were and, above all, different from them. Look, however, at what happens: we have a natural tendency to *identify* imperialism with 'colonial' or 'neo-colonialist' conquest and aggression, with the pillaging and exploitation of the Third World. All that is indeed part of what imperialism has in its hunting bag. But are we aware that imperialism operates first and foremost in the metropolitan countries, at metropolitan workers' expense? That imperialism is first and foremost a domestic (and global) matter before it is a matter of foreign interventions?

Things must therefore be clear.

For Lenin, imperialism is capitalism's 'supreme stage', its 'ultimate', 'culminating' stage, in an extremely precise sense. It is the last stage in the history, that is, the existence, of capitalism. Afterwards it's all over: no more capitalism. Afterwards it's the proletarian revolution, the dictatorship of the proletariat and the construction of socialism. Afterwards there begins the very long 'transition' that should bring us from capitalism to communism: the construction of socialism, precisely, paving the way for the transition to communism.

But beware! When Lenin says that imperialism is the last stage of capitalism and that afterwards it's all over, we must realize

1. that this last stage can last a long time; and

2. that afterwards we will find ourselves facing an alternative; afterwards it is '*either* socialism *or* barbarism'. This phrase is taken from Marx and Engels.[1] It means that history does not tend 'naturally' and automatically towards socialism, for history is not pursuing the realization of a goal, as all idealists believe. It means that if circumstances are favourable, that is, if the proletarian class struggle has been well conducted, if it is well conducted, *then* and *then alone* can the end of capitalism culminate in revolution and socialism, leading to communism by way of the long march of the 'transition'. Otherwise, the end of capitalism can lead

to 'barbarism'. What is barbarism? Regression while remaining in place, stagnation while remaining in place, of a kind of which human history offers examples by the hundreds. Yes, our 'civilization' can perish in place, not only without rising to a higher 'stage' or sinking to a lower stage that has already existed, but in accumulating all the suffering of a childbirth that will not end, of a stillbirth that is not a delivery.[2]

[On the Marxists' Relation to Marx's Work]

What I would like to expound is, in the end, *very simple*. If we have a tendency to consider it very complicated or even 'complex' (a word which, although it is all the rage in the Party, only serves to foreclose all explanation when the subject is the least bit unsettling), that tendency is the effect of a cause which is itself very simple, at least in principle. It is not because Marx's explanations are complicated, nor is it because Marx, who had, on his own, to *tear himself away from* the enormous mass of bourgeois ideology pressing down on him, to take precautions by the thousands, to guard against dangers right and left and arm himself with every possible argument. No. For it has been more than one hundred years since Marx wrote *Capital*. More than one hundred years in which to read it, clear up the problems in it and correct its inevitable mistakes. (Of all the scientists who founded a science, which one did not utter a few inanities in setting out on [his] giant's task?) More than one hundred years to understand it, quite simply.

What use has been made, in this respect (understanding *Capital*), of those one hundred years? One that is, on careful consideration, strange, disconcerting, unprecedented and, in many respects, stupefying. For if *Capital*'s main teachings have plainly been integrated into the proletarian class struggle, into labour unions and proletarian parties (that is by far the most important thing, politically speaking), we have to admit that our understanding of *Capital* has made precious little progress.

What did the Second International's great intellectuals – I do not just mean Kautsky, a non-negligible Marxist (see *The Agrarian Question*)[3] or Bernstein, who was open to challenge very early on, but even Mehring[4] (who wrote a life of Marx)[5] and Rosa Luxemburg (who must, however, be treated with special consideration, for, Lenin *dixit*, she was an 'eagle')[6] – what did these great intellectuals, generally academics with wide experience in reading, explaining and even producing commentaries on texts, make of *Capital*? As far as reading goes, they read it, certainly better than anyone else, and in any case better than the Marxists of our generation. They read it, but *they did not understand it*. They fell short of the *Capital* they read. Lenin had to tell us why: they read it as Marxist academics. They did not read it from the standpoint of the proletariat's theoretical class positions. Hence, they read it from theoretical class positions that were (more or less) bourgeois.

The only person to have read *Capital* (very young) and understood it (straightaway) was Lenin. His early texts bear witness to this. He made no mistake about what he read. Right away, he grasped the class meaning of Marx's work and understood that, to understand *Capital*, one had to read it from class theoretical and political positions. Hence the extraordinary textual commentaries in Lenin's first essays, in which he forcibly brought to the Populists' and other romantic economists' attention the elementary truth that Marx is not Political Economy, but the critique of Political Economy: that is to say, above all, the critique of economism, because economism alone believes that Political Economy is Political Economy.

Lenin, however, was not just the one reader truly faithful to Marx, the one reader of *Capital* truly faithful to *Capital*. He 'developed Marxist theory'. He wrote in one of his early works, precisely (*What the Friends of the People Are*), that 'Marx's theory ... has only laid the foundation stone of the science which socialists must develop in all directions'.[7] Lenin was then thinking (he says so explicitly here) of the concrete analysis of each Western country – but he was also thinking further than that. And he proved what he said, not just in the field of the practice of the class struggle, where he put forward decisive new theses, but also in the field of theory, where he gave us very important philosophical theses (the decisive link, unequal development and so on), and in the field of historical materialism, where he gave us the theory of imperialism (if in very schematic form, on his own admission).

Lenin himself, however, did not alter Marx in the least. In a passage of *What is To Be Done?*, I believe it is, he says he is *in favour of revising Marxism*, for every science has to be corrected, for every science is 'infinite' and, consequently, must begin with necessarily imperfect formulas, which one must know how to correct as one goes along. And he cites Mehring (the man whose name I was trying to recall) as an example of a Marxist who corrected certain inaccurate affirmations of Marx's (probably affirmations about *history*).[8] Lenin says: Mehring was right to revise Marx, because he did so *while taking all possible scientific precautions*. To this, Lenin opposes Bernstein's pseudo-revision, which is merely a lapse into bourgeois ideology. Thus, Lenin recognized in principle (citing Mehring's example) that the science founded by Marx has *necessarily to be corrected* in order to pursue its life as a science. Otherwise, it would no longer be science, but a collection of formulas and recipes fallen from the rank of the sciences.

Yet Lenin, who extended Marxist science with the theory of imperialism, *never corrected a single formula of Marx's* after declaring that it was inaccurate and in need of correction for such-and-such a reason. Is this entirely accurate? No. For we observe that Lenin felt free not to use certain *philosophical* formulas of Marx's in his own work. This was, no doubt, a way of judging them inappropriate, since he did not take them up. It was a criticism, if one likes, but a criticism that did not state its reasons, perhaps because Lenin considered them blindingly obvious. (For example, the category of *alienation*, the pride and joy of our bourgeois Marxologists and even many communist Marxists today, a category still present in *Capital*, disappears *completely* in Lenin: obviously, he does not need it in order to understand *Capital*.)

If, however, we leave this symptomatic silence aside, while noting that it is a silence that does not state its reasons, we have to admit that *Lenin never criticized-corrected a single theoretical formula of Marx's*. Lenin himself, who wrote that it was natural to rectify Marxism (even to revise it) on this or that mistaken, and necessarily mistaken, point – for, however great a genius he was, Marx was just a man, and a man who lays the foundations of a new science, caught up as he is in the ideology from which he has to free himself in order to found it, is highly likely to remain attached to certain erroneous or partial views – Lenin himself did not apply his own clear principle. He took Marx as he presented himself. He understood Marx admirably, but *changed nothing* essential in him. If he abandoned this or that philosophical category that seemed to him to be obviously superfluous or mistaken, Lenin corrected none of Marx's scientific concepts and none of the scientific results of Marx's scientific work.

If Lenin did not allow himself this audacity or, rather – for in this case we cannot speak of audacity: this simple right, let us even say *duty* towards the science founded by Marx – what shall we say of his successors? Gramsci alone, perhaps, sensed this necessity, and sensed that it was *vitally important* to rework some of Marx's findings. Rather than certain formulas of Marx's, however, he criticized his successors' formulas, *philosophical* formulas, for the most part (Engels, Bukharin's Manual).[9] Yet, to my knowledge, Gramsci, who, like Lenin, ventured onto terrain poorly explored by Marx (in Gramsci's case, the field of the superstructure), did not correct Marx's scientific formulations themselves. Moreover, Gramsci's imprisonment denied him access to the major texts. This makes itself felt in his *Prison Notebooks*: *Capital* is practically absent in them (although, curiously, the Preface to the *Contribution* [*to the Critique of Critical Economy*] recurs incessantly, as do the Theses on Feuerbach). Thus, if Lenin and Gramsci refused to perform this *duty*, what shall we say of Lenin's successors, Gramsci's contemporaries, or their present-day epigones? Of course, they, for their part, 'revise' Marx and *Capital* and the labour-theory of value and reject, like our Aron,[10] the theory of surplus value and, generally, all the principles of historical materialism. Then, however, we find ourselves in the situation that Lenin discussed: as far as revision of Marxism and rigorous, incontestable scientific rectification of it on one or another point go, fine! But if that revision is an open or disguised, total or partial way of throwing Marxism overboard, then nothing more need be said: we have nothing in common with these gentlemen. And it's perfectly pointless to say anything more on the subject.

Yet that is the stupefying situation we find ourselves facing. We have no end of 'revisions' of Marxism that are so many liquidations of Marxism: serious revisions, subtle revisions, sentimental revisions, vulgar revisions and even crude revisions – revisions for every taste. But as for 'revisions' of Marxism that would be so many *scientific rectifications*, precise, limited (to this or that concept, this or that question), argued, proven and incontestable, *we quite simply don't have any*.

I repeat: we have 'developments' of Marxism involving one or another 'object' (for example, imperialism, by Lenin), one or another domain (for example, the super-structure, by Gramsci). These 'developments' of Marxism are plainly enrichments of Marxist theory, no question about it. Nor is there any question of denying that these theoretical enrichments (for example, Lenin's theory of imperialism) have also had phenomenal practical conse-quences in the field of the conduct of the proletarian class struggle (and proletarian internationalism). These developments, however, *can by no means be called scien-tific rectifications* of Marx's formulations. Bourgeois critics spend their time saying that Marx was mistaken. That's their business and it's only to be expected (we might perhaps have an interest in occasionally lending an ear to what the most serious among them have to say, a critical ear, but let us not go into that). However, *no Marxist has ever said that this or that scientific formula of Marx's was mistaken* – no Marxist has ever shown that such-and-such a formula of Marx's was ambiguous and ought to be corrected and replaced with another.

There we have the history of our relations with Marx's scientific work. Yet, at the same time, we assert that Marx founded a science and, in making the assertion, we affirm by the same token that, if Marx's theory is not a philosophy (a philosophy does not have to be corrected to live), but a *science*, it must, quite simply to live as a science, be corrected on certain precise points. Thus we are advocates and representatives of a science to which, for one hundred years and more, we have not rendered the elementary service of correcting the least of its concepts, the least of its formulations, the least of its inaugural arguments! A strange way to serve this science! This may help explain some of the scientific difficulties in which we find ourselves and some of the scientific obstacles we butt up against, to say nothing of the objections and replies in which we get entangled. To say nothing, as well, of the imaginary theories we invent to account for these dead ends.

Imaginary theories? Let us say a few words about one of the most astonishing. To justify their theoretical (philosophical and scientific) helplessness and also lend themselves the corresponding political good conscience (for everyone knows that when a Christian runs up against a serious difficulty in our three-dimensional space, he bails out by way of the fourth dimension, Heaven; similarly, when certain Marxists butt up against a theoretical difficulty in our wretched three-dimensional space, they bail out by way of the fourth dimension: politics!), certain Marxists, under the Second International, to begin with, and then under the Third, came up with the splendid idea that Marx's theory was a *philosophy*. Yet Marx and Engels had declared a hundred times over that *Capital* was a scientific work. Lenin repeated this and explained it without the least ambiguity in *What the 'Friends of the People' Are*: Marx had founded a *science*, a very special kind of science, to be sure, because it is revolutionary, but a science. Lenin explained that, like all sciences, it is *experimental*; that, like every experimental science, it is based on the *repetition* of phenomena, brings a system of abstract concepts into play and provides, through experimentation, objectively proven results that are incontestable (except for those who, for class reasons, do not care to see them).[11]

Do you suppose that Marx's and Engels's insistent, oft-repeated declarations or Lenin's detailed explanations carried some weight? Not a bit of it! For once, people did not handle the classic texts with kid gloves, but purely and simply dismissed all these embarrassing positions as 'scientistic' (Marx and Engels, the poor fellows, had obviously lived in a period of epistemological obscurantism) and affirmed, as simply as could be, that Marxist theory was at bottom a philosophy (there is already something of this in Labriola, who was a great thinker) or purely and simply philosophy (the thesis of Lukács, Korsch, Révai and others). Do you suppose that this position has disappeared together with these big or little names? Not at all. It has been trimmed to fit our modernity, and people tell us and write in the most official texts, current even today, twenty years after the death of Stalin, who developed this formula, that 'historical materialism is an integral part of dialectical materialism'. Either words are meaningless or else they mean the following: Marxist science is an integral part of the (Marxist) philosophy which bears the name dialectical materialism.

What is a science which is an integral part of a philosophy, if not, in the best of cases, a department of philosophy? And what is a department ('an integral part', hence a 'component') of philosophy, if not philosophy? It has the appearance of a science, perhaps, but one unaware that it is philosophy. Since the same authorized authors simultaneously declare that the philosophy in question is 'scientific', they are very ill-at-ease when they have to think what difference there might be between a science that is 'an integral part of philosophy' and the aforementioned 'scientific' philosophy! For them, however, the problem is not to *think* what they say, it is to *say* what they think, even if they cannot think what they think. And they have to say what they say, precisely, in order to face up to the improbable situation that they accept as *natural*: the existence of a science that there can be no question of altering in the slightest; above all, a science whose least little concept must not be corrected; a science that is kept sealed away in the Books of the Classics, embalmed like the corpse of poor Lenin, the Kremlin mausoleum's helpless prisoner.

There you have an imaginary theory: Marxist theory is a philosophy, historical materialism is 'an integral part of dialectical materialism'. And here is what this imaginary theory is good for: if Marxist science is a philosophy, since a philosophy does not need to be rectified to live, there's no need to rectify Marxist science! Prohibition on rectifying Marxist science! Or rather (for each of the two explanations is simply the reverse side of the other): if we have been living for one hundred years face-to-face with Marx and *Capital* without ever having altered [*touché*] anything in them, or touched up [*retouché*] anything in them, it is because there is nothing to touch up in a theory which, at bottom, is not a science, but a philosophy, or an 'integral part' of Marxist philosophy.

To this imaginary solution (there are others, which objectively fulfil the same function), we should, after all, oppose a real, verifiable explanation. Let us go right to the heart of matters. If we have maintained this strange, stupefying relationship to *Capital* for one hundred years, it is because of the class struggle. We need to come to an agreement about that struggle here. We are far too inclined, when we talk about it, to suppose that what is in question is the class struggle of the proletariat and its allies. Since we take part in its struggle and have a stake in its victory, this is only to be expected. But we are in danger of forgetting the bourgeois class struggle. Above all, we are in danger of forgetting that, except when the relation of forces is reversed, the bourgeoisie holds the overall initiative in the class struggle; in other words, the bourgeois class struggle is the more powerful. What is called the domination of the class in power is reflected in the preponderance of the bourgeois class struggle over the proletarian class struggle.

The bourgeoisie wages its implacable class struggle by all available means, legal and illegal, in *the economic base* (production and exchange), dominated by forms of oppression tailored to the extortion of absolute and relative surplus value, and, at the same time, in the super-structure: by means of the repressive state apparatus and the various ideological state apparatuses (including the political apparatus – bourgeois 'democracy'– but also the Church, the School System and so on). When we consider the bourgeois class struggle, we are too often inclined to evoke only the repressive state apparatus and bourgeois democracy's 'political system'. We neglect the bourgeois class struggle in the economic base, whose terrible reality the workers know well, as well as the bourgeois class struggle in 'ideology'.

Why these reminders? In order to explain that once the workers' movement had been fitted out with Marx's theory, it had other tasks than that of rectifying *Capital*. It had, first of all, to defend itself against the bourgeoisie's redoubled assaults and the general reaction that followed the Paris Commune, and patiently to construct workers' parties. Once these parties had been constructed, however, once intellectuals of great value had been recruited, such as those of the Second International and Third International, once the intellectuals of the workers' movement who were the great leaders of these Internationals had been theoretically trained, once intellectuals with unimpeachable academic training had been recruited, first under the Second International and then, after its treason, under the Third and thereafter, how do we explain the fact that a task vital for Marxist science was *constantly deferred* – the task of going back to the beginnings of Marx's science, examining its concepts and formulas and correcting them where needed?

There is something like a mystery here, one I do not claim to have solved, but about which I would like to propose a *partial* hypothesis. I say partial, because it is hard, given the present state of the documentation and information at our disposal (this second deficiency is another astonishing fact) – it is hard to say whether the partial 'cause' I just evoked is not itself one 'effect' of a more general political situation. That is why I say a 'mystery', and in this sense – in the sense of a reality all the reasons for which we cannot at present bring to light, not in the sense of a phenomenon which, by its nature, must remain forever impenetrable.

I shall therefore say the following (a partial explanation): it seems to me that the relation of forces in the ideological class struggle was such that the intellectuals of the workers' movement (its leaders and others) were subjected, in their theoretical position, and profoundly subjected, even if it was despite themselves, to the influence of bourgeois ideology. This hypothesis is not idle chatter: it can be backed up by a number of substantial, impressive facts. To consider *just this one* aspect, Marx's most important scientific revolution in *Capital* consists in the demonstration that to understand the laws governing the phenomena we call 'economic', we have to proceed by way of the absolute precondition of a radical 'Critique' of 'Political Economy', that is, of the bourgeois, idealist, abstract, eternitarian, short-sighted and, finally, mistaken conception of those phenomena (even when Political Economy put forward a few explanations that were accurate in their details).

We must beware of these words – idealism, eternitarianism, abstraction and so on, which were used to describe, after Marx himself, who employed them, the bourgeois conception of the economy with which he broke – we must beware of these words when we utter them. For they are remarkably impoverished and any intelligent bourgeois economist can just as easily adopt them for his own purposes. Here we have, precisely, a case in which, even as we use Marx's words, we have to *make them say something*, completing them or, if one prefers, replacing them with others.

For it is not enough to say that the bourgeois conception is idealist, eternitarian and the like in order to understand what Marx says. What Marx says is not the reverse side or negation or inversion of the bourgeois conception. Marx says something *completely different*, something that has nothing to do with the bourgeois conception. Marx criticizes Political Economy (the bourgeois conception of it) in order to say the following: to understand the phenomena that are called economic (he keeps the word), we have to understand them, first of all, as phenomena of the 'base' (or infrastructure).

But what is the 'base' of a mode of production? It is the unity of the productive forces and the relations of production *under the dominance of the relations of production*. First consequence: economic phenomena are intelligible not in and of themselves, but by way of relations, the relations of production, which are ultimately *class relations* established around the possession and non-possession [*la détention et la non-détention*] of the means of production. But to say class relations is to say class struggle. In a nutshell, this is what Marx says and what Political Economy finds utterly intolerable: the key to economic phenomena is the relations of production. But the relations of production are class relations, which bring on stage the capitalist class, which possesses the means of production, and the working class, which is deprived of them and sells its labour-power, exploited by the capitalist class.

From whatever angle we look at it, we come to the same conclusion: the class struggle is present in person at the very heart of economic phenomena. Whether we say that the relations of production are class relations because they bring on stage, with respect to the means of production, the two big classes of capitalist society, or whether we say that the capitalist relation of production is the relation of the sale of labour-power, that is, the relation of exploitation of labour-power, we find the classes again (the one that sells labour-power and the one that buys it to exploit it); we find the two classes again and therefore their struggle. For there can be no classes without class struggle.

There we have what one discovers in Marx when one goes beyond the formulas of the 'Critique of Political Economy' (idealism, eternitarianism and so on): the class struggle.

Thanks to Marx, we can now say so as plainly as that. Marx said so, but he went into all the details of a technical demonstration, examining the material forms of existence of economic phenomena without neglecting any of their variations. In the aridity of part of Volume Two and Volume Three of *Capital*, some have lost sight of the 'thread of the argument'. Others have lost their way in *Capital*'s laborious and often infelicitous opening section. Bourgeois economists, however, have not been fooled, by and large, and have unleashed all the forces of their intelligence against Marx. Is there any need to recall that the counter-attack was prepared in Marx's lifetime, and that Engels endeavoured to contain the first assaults, those of marginalism and that of Walras and company? Is there any need to recall that this counter-attack, which sought to restore Political Economy in its purity, technicity, neutrality and marvellously psychological 'humanity', was coupled with other attacks in the fields of philosophy, history and politics? This vast offensive, this phenomenal offensive of the bourgeois ideological class struggle, waged in the publishing industry, the press and academia, and pursued by all the non-Marxist or anti-Marxist elements of a still poorly educated workers' movement, was probably not without influence on the 'intellectuals' charged with defending Marxist theory – especially in view of the fact that a good many of them were then, and many more are today, marked by the bourgeois ideology doled out to them, in all 'neutrality' and 'laicity', by the ideological state apparatus of the school system and the university.

If this hypothesis is even partially right, it can shed light on what must be termed the form of defence that Marx's theoretical work has taken for the last one hundred years. A defence during a retreat [*en retraite*] for some – for a number of the Second International's theorists, who had read *Capital*, yet, all too often, had proposed an 'economistic' interpretation of it. It is not that they had gone back over to bourgeois Economy or bourgeois economism: with an ingenuity worthy of a better cause, they defended economistic positions *in Marxism*, by neglecting, for example, to say that the unity of the productive forces and relations of production takes place *under the dominance of* the relations of production; by saying, for example, that the economy depends on the relations of production, while failing to emphasize that the relations of production were class relations, or that there is no class without class struggle and so on. Other theorists, whom we have come to know since then, confined themselves to a *subdued* [*en retrait*] defence of Marx's theoretical works. They drew attention to their existence, when required, in essays which they published and sold, and they let slip no opportunity to say that Marx had spoken the truth, citing him at length – but as a *guarantee*. For the rest, they did not lift their little finger to correct a single one of Marx's formulas, any more than their predecessors had; and if someone ventured to do so, they were immediately on their guard. To be sure, they were not in danger of 'revising' Marx the way Bernstein did (others saw to that, in another mode). There is, however, no relying on them to correct Marx where he is mistaken or where his terms are ambiguous or where his formulas are not the best, as Lenin agreed that we should.

It is not a question of individuals here, of course, although the individuals exist; it is a question, rather, of a historical state of affairs. Nevertheless, what history can explain, history can also undo. And we have doubtless arrived at a day in which the development of the class struggle (that of the proletariat + the oppressed peoples) has, in the crisis of imperialism, attained a level such that what was only recently, if not impossible and unthinkable, then at least difficult, is becoming possible and necessary. The proof is the simple fact that we can pose this question publicly and openly at the heart of a Communist party, and pose it while suggesting elements [of an answer] (even if they are only provisional, because they will have to be 'rectified').

It remains to see what will be made of this now open possibility.

[What Is a Mode of Production?]

For the theory of the revolution and the transition to communism, the crucial point is that *the socialist mode of production* does not exist.[12]

1. The socialist mode of production does not exist.

2. The capitalist mode of production exists and the communist mode of production exists.

3. Lenin

a. never talks about the socialist mode of production, but

b. talks about socialism (which is not a mode of production) as the transition between the capitalist mode of production and the communist mode of production.

c. He defines this transition, this 'socialist socio-economic' formation, as the contradictory co-existence of the capitalist mode of production and the communist mode of production – thus as the co-existence of capitalist elements and communist elements, of elements of the communist mode of production and of the capitalist mode of production.

4. Hence the question: *when does communism* begin to exist, understood as elements (or seeds, but seeds in the sense of seeds capable of producing elements)?[13] Answer: from the moment the capitalist mode of production exists. This answer is, however, too generic, and is abstract. Yet it means (a thesis defended by Marx) that the capitalist mode of production contains the seeds of the communist mode of production in its own contradictions from the moment it comes into existence. More precisely, we can say that communism exists (begins to exist in a real sense) with the earliest developments of the workers' class struggle. Look at what Marx says in the [1844] *Manuscripts* about the French workers: society is no longer a means to an end, but a need.[14] Look at everything Marx says about the disintegration of capitalist forms of the family, religion and so on.[15]

The capitalist mode of production, which emerges on and from the decay of pre-capitalist modes of production (not just feudal, but other modes of production as well, and not just where there is no feudalism – for example, the Asiatic mode of production, the lineage-based mode of production,[16] or the vestiges of the slave-based mode of production), itself decays from the moment it emerges, for a simple reason: the antagonism of the capitalist relation of production. This antagonism exists from the origin on and, from the origin on, produces effects of decomposition because of its antagonism (class struggle), which affects the forms of existence of the capitalist mode of production (division of labour, organization of labour, the family and other ideological state apparatuses).

The history of capitalism must be regarded as a process that is contradictory from its beginnings (because of the antagonistic nature of the capitalist relation of production). On the one hand, it creates its own forms and, at the same time, these very forms start decaying; on the one hand, it *strengthens* its own forms (consider how much time it needed to put the scholastic Ideological State Apparatus in place, or bourgeois democracy, or a task-based division of labour, or the labour unions intended to divide the working class, or its world hegemony based on colonial and neocolonialist exploitation); yet, at the same time, these same forms *are weakened* under the impact of the class struggle: the family disintegrates, the School System as well, religion as well; the state apparatus seizes up, and the economy, despite the post-1929 controls, runs faster than the state apparatus. (It has always run faster; but the paradox is that, having discovered, after 1929, the means of remedying crises, imperialism, after avoiding the spectacular, abrupt, catastrophic forms of the 1929 crisis, went into a crisis that is insoluble because it is controlled by the financial apparatus of so-called state monopoly capitalism.)

5. The forms in which communist elements appear in capitalist society itself are countless. Marx himself names a whole series of them, from forms of children's education combining work and schooling[17] to the new relations reigning in proletarian organizations,[18] the proletarian family,[19] the proletarian community of life and struggle,[20] joint-stock companies,[21] workers' co-operatives[22] and so on, to say nothing of the 'socialization of production', which poses all sorts of problems, yet should also be noted.[23] All these elements (which have multiplied in the past few years, especially since 1968; see LIP,[24] the proletarian inventions in the class struggle: 'they have shown that the workers could do without bosses', Séguy)[25] will

not by itself lead to communism. Better: they are not all communist elements. They are elements for communism. Communism will adopt them, combine them, perfect them and develop their potentiality [*virtualités*], integrating them into the revolution in the relations of production which commands everything and is still absent from our world. Communism, however, will not come about by itself. It has to be built at the end of a long march, one stage of which is called socialism, which is not a mode of production.

6. Whence the question: How shall we define a mode of production?

In the mistaken thesis that socialism is a mode of production, there lies concealed the idea that *every* historical socio-economic formation, since it exists, functions on the basis of a mode of production that is specific to it, original and definable.

This idea is completely mistaken.

As a function of this mistaken idea, it is said that socialism is a mode of production whose relations of production (in the plural) are constituted by 1. collective ownership of the means of production (collective ownership = state ownership) and 2. working-class state power. Thus by *two* relations.

Marx, however, never defined a mode of production by *two* relations: 1. a relation of ownership of the means of production (bearing on the infrastructure) and 2. a relation of power (bearing on the superstructure). He defined it by *one and only one relation*, the relation *of production*, the relation *specific to production*, hence a relation internal to the infrastructure. And Marx never defined *the* relation of production as an (individual or collective) *relation of ownership* of the means of production; he defined it as an antagonistic and thus double relation of the *possession and non-possession* of the means of production.

7. Marx's position is clear

a. There are not as many modes of production as there are historically existing social formations.

b. The number of social formations that have existed historically is extremely high. It is a great deal higher than the number of social formations that we know of thanks to the traces and monuments they have left behind, because a considerable number of social formations that have existed in history have disappeared, many of them without a trace.

c. The number of modes of production that have been identified to date is extremely limited. According to Marx, we know of 1) the different forms of primitive community (of which there exist transformed forms, like the one that can be called, for convenience, the lineage-based mode of production in Africa); 2) the so-called Asiatic mode of production; 3) the slave-based mode of production; 4) the feudal mode of production; 5) the capitalist mode of production and 6) the communist mode of production, which does not yet exist anywhere in the world, although we have very serious reasons for thinking that it will some day.

8. There is a glaring contradiction between the extremely high number of social formations that have existed or exist and the extremely limited number of modes of production recognized as such by Marx.

Thus it is not enough for a social formation to exist for a mode of production of its own to correspond automatically to it. This may be the case: a capitalist social formation realizes a mode of production of its own, the capitalist mode of production. This may not be the case: to a socialist social formation, there does not correspond a mode of production that would be called socialist.

The reason is simple: a social formation can fall 'between two stools', can be 'in transition' between two modes of production, without having its own, exclusive mode of production, its personal mode of production, as it were. It can participate in two modes of production, the one it is in the process of casting off and the one it is in the process of constructing. When you travel from Paris to Marseille, you do not reside, throughout your trip, in a city called the 'Mistral'. The Mistral is, precisely, a train that takes you from Paris to Marseilles. The Mistral is aptly named:[26] it whistles like the wind, and the wind has never been a city or resided in a city.

We must, in fact, go much further. Any social formation whatsoever is in transit or in transition or on a voyage in history. Even a capitalist social formation is in transition, even a social formation that truly possesses its own mode of production, authenticated, identified, guaranteed, 'all its own', such as a capitalist social formation. A capitalist social formation (in our part of the world, Western Europe) comes from feudalism and still bears within it powerful elements of the feudal mode of production (ground rent, 'independent' (!) petty producers – above all peasants, but also artisans, the people employed in 'mercantile production', as the phrase goes) and already, as we have seen, elements of communism.

We must not, however, exaggerate about transit and transition. For, in the case of a capitalist society, it is, after all, *its* mode of production that is dominant – the capitalist mode of production – and that is why we can say, because of this dominance, that a capitalist social formation realizes the capitalist mode of production. Even if we know that it realizes it at the price of dragging elements of the feudal mode of production along with it and of secreting in itself elements of the future communist mode of production, the fact is that it is dominated by the capitalist mode of production; we must refer to the capitalist mode of production in order to understand what goes on in it.

9. But then the question arises again: *What is a mode of production?* How shall we define it to avoid falling into the trap of postulating a plurality of fictive modes of production to correspond to each social formation? What objective criterion shall we provide to make it possible to define really existing modes of production while ruling out the fabrication of imaginary modes of production?

Let us examine the classic theses.

There are several definitions in Marx (no one, straightforward definition that stands by itself, yet one discerns the definitions in the way the terms are used). Marx never provided a true, concise, well thought-out definition of the mode of production. However, he often uses the term in contexts that stand as the equivalent of a definition.

It is not surprising that the question had him going round in circles, given the extraordinary novelty of what he was saying; not surprising that he felt no need to pin down his thought in a definition (not that he did not like definitions, as Engels claims,[27] for if Marx did not like definitions, or had trouble making them, I'll be hanged after having read the first section [of *Capital Volume One*]).[28] The fact is that Marx gives no cut-and-dry definition; however, he uses the term in very many different contexts that stand as the equivalent of a definition – or of *definitions*. For he proposes several.

Collected and condensed, they can be encapsulated in two definitions.

a. A mode of production is the *way* of producing, in a technical sense. This refers to the *labour process*, in which production is considered abstractly, as mobilizing the object of labour, the means of labour and the agents of labour. 'Abstractly': that is to say, abstracting from the relations of production. When we abstract from the relations of production (when we consider production as a labour process alone), what is left? The productive forces. We then have an 'abstract' conception of the mode of production (= technical, economistic and so on). But beware! Since Marx does not content himself with this 'definition', which he needs in order to think the labour process (we cannot shirk the task of thinking the labour process) – since Marx gives this definition, but completes it with a second definition, he does not lapse into technicism or economism for a single second. That should be made very clear.[29]

b. The mode of production is *the way* of producing, in the social sense. This no longer refers to the labour process (the mobilization of the productive forces), but *to the whole process of production and reproduction*. The 'way' of producing thus no longer has anything to do with the way of combining and ordering [*agencer*] the different elements of the productive forces in *the labour process*; it has everything to do with the way of distributing the means of production and agents of production (labour-power) and reproduction in the overall process of production and reproduction. What then defines the mode of production is no longer just the productive forces, but the unity of the productive forces and the relations of production *under the dominance* of the relations of production.[30]

This first definition will offend delicate sensibilities, as it must. For it puts the relations of production in the forefront, whereas a number of Marxists and even communists hold, as 'good materialists', that we have to put the productive forces in the forefront. And it is quite true that the first men acquired – after thousands, if not millions of years – the right to what we call history only by regulating their relations with nature, producing tools, inventing cattle-rearing and agriculture, iron and bronze and so on. We have not progressed far enough to know what the driving force behind the development of these rudimentary and, later, elementary productive forces was. For the societies that Marx discusses, however, there is no ambiguity. The materialist determination that Marx invokes was never that of the productive forces (except in the imagination of all the economistic Marxists, who had an interest in the matter), but that of the 'base', the infrastructure, that is, the unity of the productive forces and relations of production. (Towards the end of the Introduction to the [*Contribution*],[31] Marx says that we should very carefully think the unity of, and difference between, the two at the same time, but that it is their unity that is more important.) And, at the practical level, Marx always conceived this material unity, determinant in the last instance, as the unity of the productive forces and relations of production *under the dominance of* the relations of production. In other words: primacy of the relations of production over the unity productive forces/relations of production. This comes down to the *Manifesto*'s thesis (I am taking a shortcut) that the class struggle is the driving force [*le moteur*] of history (Engels adds, in a note: since classes have existed, which brings us back to our question about the beginnings of human 'civilization').[32]

May we proceed?

If so, the question becomes: *What are* (in a class society and, by extension, in the classless society for which we are fighting and also in the classless societies that we know in a few parts of the world) *the relations of production*?

Let us discuss only class societies for now. Otherwise, our definitions will become extremely complicated.

The relations of production are, according to the well-known (unfortunately, much too well-known) formula of Marx's Preface to *A Contribution to the Critique of Political Economy* (1859), 'definite', 'inevitable' relations, 'independent of [men's] will', into which 'men enter' [*eingehen*] on the occasion of 'the social production of their existence'.[33]

I am not going to discuss this formula (or the translation of it),[34] which once had its merits, but also has the drawback of being a fixed star in the firmament of our theoretical references, as the one carefully considered formula that Marx has given us. I shall go straight to the facts of the matter: to what we can say after having read *Capital* and Lenin.

It is true that the relations of production establish themselves on the occasion of production, which is social – but also on the occasion of reproduction. Better: they do not establish themselves on the occasion of production. They establish themselves 'in' production. What does 'they *establish themselves*' mean? The word is accurate: they establish themselves all by themselves, without asking anyone's opinion, by virtue of a necessity that has *something* to do with what Marx calls 'correspondence with the degree of development of the forces of production',[35] but nothing to do with the mechanistic functionalism that this infelicitous concept of 'correspondence' brings with it, nor with the pseudo-obviousness of the 'degree of development of the forces of production' (otherwise, since the USA's productive forces are superior to the USSR's and since its productivity is six times greater, one wonders why the relations of production in the USA have missed their 'correspondence'[36] – unless the USA is surreptitiously 'laying the foundations of communism' without first going through socialism, which would be in the style of that 'American practical-mindedness' that Lenin made so much of).

Not only do the relations of production establish

themselves *in* production; since they govern it, we must say, rather, that production and reproduction are *in* the relations of production! These little words ('in') are always troublesome when we fail to control them. Let us therefore say, to take up our first formulation again, that the relations of production are the *determinant* element in the ensemble of the processes of production and reproduction (since all social production-reproduction implies the *unity* of the forces of production/relations of production *under the dominance of* the relations of production).

The question arises again: What are the relations of production? One says (always the same old song): 'relations into which men enter …'. No; they do not enter into them the way one enters a restaurant or a political party. Men are *taken in* [*pris*] them and they are taken in them insofar as they are parties to them [*parties prenantes*],[37] but not on the same level. They are parties to them only because they are first ('first' means 'fundamentally' – it is not a question of time) *taken in them, are obliged to submit to them.* First point. 'Men'? You and me, and John, Dick and Harry?

Here we must briefly pause to ask: But *to what end* do they have to submit to them? When you have to submit to something, it's always for a reason: you submit to military service because of the law and the police; you submit on the operating table because of your appendicitis. But in the case to hand? The fact is that 'men' have to submit to the relations of production (this presupposes – Marx says as much – that it is not a question of will, freedom, a contract, a 'project' or the like) 'in relation to', if I may put it that way, the means of production.[38] The relations of production are distinguished by the fact that 1. they are not relations between men *alone*, but, like quite a few of the relations we know involving men, relations between men with respect to things, the things called means of production, precisely; relations between men with respect to the relations of these men to these things (the means of production);[39] and 2. since these are relations between men with respect to the things known as means of production, they are neither relations between men nor relations between certain men – as we shall see.

Relations between men with respect to the means of production. Not, however, just any relations! This little world is very precise, rigorous, implacable. Here is how it works. There are the means of production (in existence at time t). There are men. And, among the men, there are two categories (two classes): those who possess the means of production and the others, who possess nothing at all or possess only their labour-power. That is the situation in the capitalist mode of production.

If, however, we wish to take not just the capitalist mode of production into consideration, but also the feudal mode of production, Asiatic mode of production and slave-based mode of production, we have to go further.

10. In that case, to take up a short, brilliant sentence of Marx's in [*Capital*] Volume Three, which says about the state that 'the whole of its secret resides in the relationship between the direct producers and the means of production',[40] we may say roughly the following: the relations of production are defined by the relationship existing, *on the one hand*, between the direct producers (those who actually produce, the direct agents of the labour-process, those who have no one beneath them, those who 'get their hands dirty' and 'transform matter') and, *on the other hand*,

I. $\left\{ \begin{array}{l} \text{the means of production} \\ \text{labour-power} \end{array} \right\}$ these comprise the productive forces

II. the product,

hence by the relationship between the direct producers on the one hand and the productive forces and product on the other.[41]

We have to introduce this distinction in 'on the other hand' in order to account for the known modes of production.

Thus, *in the capitalist mode of production*, we know that the direct producers do not possess the means of production, but we believe that they possess their labour-power, since they cede it to those who possess the means of production, the capitalists, in exchange for wages. Marx, however, has done enough to show that this legal exchange, sanctioned by a contract freely accepted by the parties to it [*les parties prenantes*], like any other contract, hence accepted by the workers as well, is a swindle. Capital's wage-earners, as a class, do not possess their labour-power: it belongs in advance to capital, which reproduces it in order to exploit it on an extended scale (this is the law of population characteristic of the capitalist mode of production, one of Marx's discoveries).[42] Possessing neither the means of production nor their labour-power, the direct producers do not possess the product of the production whose agents they are.

However, since the form of non-possession of labour-power in the capitalist regime is the contract bearing on the sale of labour-power, and since this form of non-possession differs from other forms that we shall examine, it is correct to say that the capitalist relation of production is the wage relation = the relation of non-possession of the means of production and labour-power = the relation of the separation of labour-power from the means of production and so on.

In the feudal mode of production, things happen in much the same way, but with certain differences. The serf possesses his means of production (thus he appears to be an 'independent petty producer': this category is characteristic of the feudal mode of production and applies to serfs as well as urban artisans), but this possession is the form in which non-possession appears. The serf, to confine our attention to him, possesses neither his means of production (the lord's eminent domain, as feudal law states the matter) nor his labour-power (the lord consents to let him use it to produce what he needs to survive and to reproduce himself), but 1. the lord levies tributes on the products and 2. he uses labour-power for himself, on his fields, which the serf cultivates for nothing, and also for corvées (that is another question, which we shall leave aside).

Under these conditions, the serf does not possess the product: he keeps only that portion of it which the lord leaves for him. Let us note, however, that labour-power forms part of the means of production; in other words, the productive forces are compulsorily bound to their base in the land (the serf cannot leave the land to which he 'belongs'; he is possessed by the means of production that are apparently his). This is a form of non-possession, hence of dependency, which differs from capitalist non-possession in that there is no labour contract and no wage-relation: the labour-contract and the wage-relation make sense only on the basis of an economy in which commodity relations have become dominant, and that is not the case in the feudal mode of production.

The relation of production of the feudal mode of production can, accordingly, be characterized as follows: non-possession of the means of production and of labour-power by the direct producers in the form of apparent possession of the means of production (the independent petty producer), accompanied by non-possession of labour-power and of the product.

In the case of the slave-based mode of production, what is conspicuous is the radical non-possession of labour-power. The slave is bought and sold and reproduced like livestock. Non-possession of the means of production and of the product. When commodity relations are sufficiently developed in the slave-based mode of production, the slave can become an object of commercial transactions: he has a price. Commodity relations, however, bypass him, as it were, as they bypass the slave-based mode of production. We should not be fooled by the existence of commodity relations in pre-capitalist modes of production: they are always, 'like Epicurus' gods', in society's 'pores' (or on its surface), as Marx puts it; they do not penetrate the infrastructure and they do not affect the relation of production.[43] Although the slave has a price and is bought and sold on the slave market, the relation of production of the slaveholding mode of production is not a commodity relation like the relation of production of the capitalist mode of production.

As for the Asiatic mode of production (which Marx thought it indispensable *to identify* and call to his readers' attention),[44] although the research currently in progress has not produced absolutely definitive results, it seems that we can say the following.

In the Asiatic mode of production, the direct producers

work in communal fashion. They possess their means of production and their labour-power, but not their product, most of which is levied by the caste that runs the state and carries out major construction projects or wages war and so on.

To provide a uniform account of the different cases identified by Marx (the different known modes of production), therefore, we have had to mobilize the following double table:

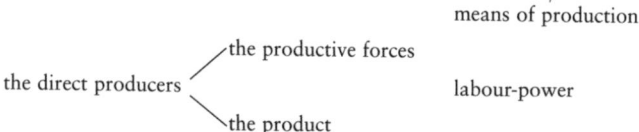

If we had left the case of the Asiatic mode of production aside, we could have left the product out of account and *brought the productive forces alone into play*.

It may be preferable to do so, for we do not know with certainty whether we should consider the Asiatic mode of production to be a mode of production of class societies.

If we do leave the Asiatic mode of production aside, we have:

1. Slave-based mode of production: the relation of production of the slave-based mode of production is *absolute non-possession* of their labour-power by the direct producers. From this there follow the absolute non-possession of the means of production and the absolute non-possession of the product.

This condition of exploitation defines a class: the slaves. At the same time, it defines another class: the slave-holders, who possess simultaneously the direct producers' labour-power, the means of production and the product. These two classes are antagonistic.

2. Feudal mode of production: the relation of production of the feudal mode of production is the direct producers' *relative non-possession of their labour-power in a form that is not a commodity form*, but 'natural' (or supposedly natural), combined with the direct producers' *relative*

non-possession of the means of production, again in a form that is said to be 'natural', that is, a non-commodity form. The consequence is relative non-possession of the product.

This condition of exploitation defines a class: the serfs (artisans, as Marx showed, are constructed on the same model: here commodity relations are non-determinant in feudalism's heyday). At the same time, it defines another class: the serfs' lords and masters, who possess, relatively, the serfs' labour-power and, eminently, their means of production. They draw their revenue from the product, supposedly in compensation for the services that they render the serfs (by protecting them from invasions by other lords, who only overrun the poor peasants' lands because they are lords whose business is with other lords and their serfs, hence in order to increase their own revenues; this reciprocal banditry is baptized 'protection of the poor peasants' by those who exploit them and, in defending them against competing lords, merely defend their own exploited human livestock); they divert the better part of the product for their own gain. These classes are antagonistic.

3. *Capitalist mode of production*: the relation of production of the capitalist mode of production is the direct producers' absolute non-possession of the means of production and relative non-possession of their labour-power. This *relative non-possession of labour-power takes the form of a commodity relation, wages*.

This condition defines a class: the proletarians. At the same time, it defines another class: the capitalists. These two classes are antagonistic.

At the end of this rapid analysis, we may say the following.

1. In the course of our exposition, we have eliminated, perhaps even unawares, the initial expression, the one Marx uses in the *Contribution* (and, of course, earlier in *The German Ideology*, *The Poverty of Philosophy* and other texts), and even most of the texts in *Capital*: the relations of production. We have replaced it with another expression: *the* relation of production.

Why this substitution? Because our experience has shown that we had no need at all for the plural and that the singular was perfectly sufficient.

As confirmation, it should be noted that Marx himself *uses the singular* in the recently translated unpublished chapter of *Capital*.[45] Apparently, our experience was the same as his.

Is this a matter of detail? Yes and no. Yes, because the plural can serve when we have to show the diversity of the effects that the relation of production of a mode of production can have, all the more so in that, to a certain extent, the effects of the relation of production of a mode of production comprise *other relations*, which are, to be sure, not the relation of *production* (they can be relations of circulation, distribution or exchange, political, ideological, legal relations and so on), but are nonetheless *relations*.

It is enough to say so, however, to see right away the confusion into which the expression 'relations of production' *in the plural* can plunge the reader. For while these other relations, which depend on the relation of production, are plainly relations, they are not relations of production! If one imagines that they are, one can make very serious mistakes. For example, one can suppose that the relations of production are *property* relations, that is, *legal* relations. But legal relations, *property* relations in particular, are not relations of production. On this point, despite all the accumulated inanities, we have to re-establish the truth of Marx's texts. Marx never said that the relations of production were property relations in the legal sense of the term 'property'. Even if he may occasionally have let the word slip, there are enough passages in which he spells out what he thinks to rule out all ambiguity. Thus it is that, beginning with the *Contribution*, if it is read closely, Marx distinguishes *Besitz*, de facto possession, from *Eigentum* (de jure property). It is clear that, *beginning with the Contribution* (a text that is, moreover, still in search of its theoretical moorings), Marx holds that the capitalist relation of production has to do with *Besitz* (de facto possession and non-possession), not with *Eigentum* (legal, de jure property, property to which title is held).

Another counter-example (I could adduce a great many, but shall limit myself): to talk about relations of production *in the plural* and about *social* relations of production to boot (as if there existed non-social relations in the matter that Marx discusses!) is to grant oneself a splendidly convenient plural, after all. Once one has shown one's colours, announcing this solemn, programmatic plural with great fanfare, nothing is easier than to beef it up, either by stuffing everything that comes one's way into the relations of production (*social* relations, if you please) or by nursing the firm impression that, come what may, one is on the right track. For example, it is in the name of this marvellously facile solution that one exempts oneself from the obligation to become personally acquainted with *the other relations*, those which are not 'of production': relations of circulation, distribution, consumption (Now how about that! In our good old 'consumer society'! Which of our worthy Marxists has ever taken it into his head that there exist relations of consumption? And that they vary with the different modes of production?), together with legal relations (Now how about that! Why have Marxists left the theory of law undeveloped since poor Pashukanis,[46] who is doubtless not satisfied with being dead, as everyone knows, since communists come to spit on his tomb in the name of their notion of the Marxist theory of law – more precisely, because they need to assure themselves that that theory has already been forged or that there is no reason for it to exist or that it comes under the – relations of production!)[47] and also political relations and ideological relations (Now how about that! Why has the Marxist theory of the superstructure been at a standstill for years, to the point that all that was said, after all, by Gramsci, who *did* concern himself with it, has practically remained a dead letter?). I shall not insist. The phrase 'the relations of production' has sheltered, under its plural, not just very grave illogicalities (the idea that the relations of production are legal relations, property relations), but also – how to put it so as not to hurt anyone's feelings?

– all the casual complicities of the Marxist understanding of the world.

Hence the interest of the singular. *The* relation of production.

2. Second remark. It is clear, after what has been said about the direct producers and their relation to the productive forces (means of production, labour-power) that everything is played out, wholly, exclusively, in the infrastructure; better, in that part of the infrastructure known as *production.* (Is there any need to repeat that the infrastructure also includes circulation, exchange, distribution and consumption?)

That is one more reason to stick to our singular. For our good 'pluralist' friends ask for nothing better than a chance to explain to us that the relation*s* of production are a 'complex' business; and, under the cover provided by this contraband adjective, they fob whatever they like off on us in order to 'flesh out' these meagre relations of production somewhat, to fatten them up with relations of circulation and exchange, monetary relations and legal relations, that is, the political and ideological relations they have in their heads – the last-named relations with no relation to reality!

Conclusion: we shall make no concessions on this singular. It is a point of non-return, for it is an anchor point of Marx's materialism and an anchor point of the class struggle as well.

3. As we have seen, each relation of production in each mode of production defines two classes, two antagonistic classes. Here we can at last settle the much vexed question of 'men'.

Everyone knows this old song. The relations of production are 'relations between men'. Since someone happens to have pointed out (in 1965) 1. that these relations between men are not human relations; 2. are not 'intersubjective'; 3. are not just relations between men, inasmuch as things, the means of production, are at stake; and 4. are therefore, above all, relations and so on,[48] one says today (Lucien Sève) that although they are not inter-human relations, they are nonetheless relations between men.[49] Okay. The old song continues.

We even know Marx's old song: 'In the social production of their existence, men inevitably enter (*eingehen*) (says the translation published by Éditions sociales) into [*sic*][50] necessary relations'. ... If men 'enter into relations', it must be that they were outside to begin with, hence men like you and me who, one fine day, take the step. Voluntarily? Not necessarily. They can be forced to. When you are forced to do something, you are no less a man for that.

Marx's truth is as follows (I leave to one side interpretation of the famous sentence from the *Contribution*). The relations of production are not relations between certain men, or between men, but relations between classes. Or, to stick to our singular, which is decisive in this matter too, *the* relation of production (in the singular) is not a relation (Do you see how the plural works here too? 'Men' is in the plural, is it not? What could be more natural than to put the relations of production in the plural to match it?) between men or certain men who exist prior to it: it is a *relation between classes* that are defined and constituted by the relation of production itself. For, in comparison with men, the classes at least have the advantage of leaving no doubt about the fact that they do not exist prior to the relation of production.

One should reread Marx if one does not know this, for it means that one has failed to understand one of the most important things he has given us. For, after all, the idea that the social classes are made up of men, that the relations of production are relations between men and so on is quite simply the return of classical bourgeois ideology (whose first great theorist, and the master of all of Political Economy, was Locke, according to Marx)[51] *in Marxism.*[52] It is the way bourgeois ideology imagines social classes and the class struggle.

Remember that Marx himself said, solemnly, that it wasn't he, but bourgeois thinkers who discovered the social classes and the struggle of the classes.[53] Before the Marxist theory of classes, there was (and still is, and it is *dominant*, and weighs terribly on the communists themselves) a *bourgeois* theory of classes and the class struggle. This bourgeois theory of classes has it that classes are made up of men, that men '*enter* into relations of production' and, transformed by their meat grinder, leave them in the form of classes. First men, then relations of production, then classes, then class struggle. That is the bourgeois conception, the bourgeois theory of classes and of (bourgeois ideologues are in favour of the plural!) *social relations*. When bourgeois theorists, spurred on by the little squabbles that opposed the two rival exploiting classes, feudal and bourgeois, take theoretical audacity to the point of recognizing classes and the struggle of the classes, that is how things happen. First men, of course; come now! *Then* the social relations between men (there we have the whole history of the theory of human society put forward by natural law philosophy), *then* social classes (born of the violation of morality and law, or of the thirst for gold and so on – a perversion, but what can you do?), *and then* the upshot of the whole affair, the struggle of the classes.

One has to be aware that they never stop singing this old song to us in one variant or another; when silence reigns, this tune continues to ring in our ears. We have grown up in it and it holds us fast at the gut level, like all the other themes of bourgeois ideology; Marx had radically to sever himself from it to become Marx. Are we sufficiently aware of the fact that it continues and that many Marxists do not realize that they are chanting even Marx's formulas (including this or that early, still shaky formula) to the tune of this bourgeois song? Are we sufficiently aware of the fact that we still have to, and will always have to, tear ourselves away from this old song that bears down on us with all the weight of the bourgeoisie and its economic, political and ideological class struggle?

But are we aware that the bourgeoisie wages the class struggle? I am convinced that there are communists – yes, communists – for whom only the working class wages the class struggle, against the bourgeoisie, of course; but the bourgeoisie is capitalism and capitalism is a despicable regime standing in its place like an immense edifice which must be demolished, to be sure, and which defends itself, to be sure, but which is a sort of thing, a mountain that must be moved, from which riot police and speeches come now and then. Yet the idea that the bourgeoisie spends its time attacking, that this system is nothing but a system of class struggle, that all this holds together thanks to the bourgeois class struggle alone, that from the start and forever thereafter, the bourgeoisie has edified its reign by means of class struggle, its own class struggle, that it continues to do so, and that, for the time being, its class struggle is the more powerful, which is why we have not overturned it yet – even certain communists are not aware of all this. They have not understood the ultimate, that is, the first consequences of the *Manifesto*'s formula: 'the class struggle is the driving force of history', 'history is the history of class struggle'.

Thus there is nothing surprising about the fact that the bourgeois class struggle achieves this result, that certain communists believe it is enough to repeat Marx's words – saying that there are first men, then relations of production (that sounds good and Marxist), then classes, then the struggle of the classes – in order to be Marxists. When communists say that, the bourgeoisie has won. And it triumphs discreetly, you know. Unlike others, it contents itself with its victory; it feels no need to issue communiqués, like some of our little organizations that survive only by publishing communiqués that are not even about the victories they have won, since they only have defeats, dissolutions and arrests to chew on, but are about their failures, proclaimed victories in their communiqués.[54] These little organizations, unlike the bourgeoisie, are eloquent in defeat. However, when the bourgeoisie succeeds in passing off its old song about the classes or social relations again, it knows it's a good investment. The results always prove it.

We'll have to resign ourselves to it, then: *the relation of production* that defines a mode of production is a relation between classes – very precisely, *between the classes that this relation constitutes*; still more precisely, *between the antagonistic classes that it constitutes*. In class social formations, of course, not in classless societies.

The case of classless 'societies' or, rather, classless social formations, does not present any problems. The relation of production defining them is always identical to the relation between the direct producers and the productive forces (means of production, labour-power). Obviously, for there to be no classes, this relation must be a relation of the direct producers' *possession* of the means of production and their own labour-power. From the moment that this relation is a relation of possession (rather than being, as in all class social formations, a relation of absolute or relative non-possession in this or that form, a 'natural' form or a commodity form), there are no more classes – since it is non-possession which divides the classes into classes (I intentionally write 'which divides the classes into classes', not 'men into classes', for the latter expression is meaningless, whereas the former expression plainly says what it means: the division into antagonistic classes is identical to the constitution of the classes).

The question one can ask is the following: just as there exist different forms of non-possession (we have reviewed them), so it is a very good wager that there exist different forms of possession – to put things clearly, different forms of organization of the *communal* or *communist relation* of production in classless social formations. The fact that Marx and Engels took so great an interest in 'primitive' societies and 'primitive communism' shows that they had a presentiment that there exist both common grounds and possible variations, of which history offered them examples. And these examples from the past were not without interest for the future. It is not a question of reviving the myth of a primitive communism supposed to serve as a model for the communism to come – of nostalgically reviving the communal forms of so-called 'primitive' societies. The historical facts at least proved, however, that classless societies had existed, that a classless society can exist. This is crucial, for, inasmuch as the communist mode of production does not exist, how can one talk about it, given that Marx, a rigorous disciple of Spinoza's on this point as on so many others, talks only about what exists? The answer is that Marx can talk about it because 1. classless societies have existed; 2. the tendential development of the antagonism that haunts the capitalist mode of production (the class struggle in capitalism) prepares the advent of a classless society; 3. this classless society will be the reality of a mode of production defined by its relation of production, which will be the *possession* of the productive forces by the direct producers; and 4. this communal possession *will have to do without any commodity relations at all*, since commodity relations are historically bound up with all the class societies and since the relation of production has become a commodity relation in the capitalist mode of production.

That is about all that one can say, together with a certain number of things about all the consequences bearing on the forms of the division of labour (a 'by-product' of non-possession). We will have to discover the rest in constructing it.

11.[55] The consequences of what has just been said are plain as far as the non-existence of the socialist mode of production is concerned. Before [coming to them], however, I would like to say a word or two about the concept of 'mercantile production', the 'mercantile mode of production' and the 'independent petty producer'. These are decisive points.

A spectre or, rather, a phantom has been haunting the Marxist world for a long time now, and even since *Capital*, which has been poorly read and poorly understood, or sometimes too well read to be understood: the phantom of the independent petty producer, which drags another phantom in its wake, that of mercantile production, which drags another phantom in *its* wake, that of the mercantile mode of production. In sum, a whole train of phantoms.

Let us take a rather close look at this impressive procession.

To do so, let us begin at the end, by exorcising the pseudo-concept of the mercantile mode of production. There is no mercantile mode of production. Rather, there would be one if bourgeois ideology had arrived at the concept of the mode of production in bourgeois ideology. Since bourgeois ideology, however, will not be troubled by one Marxist concept more or less, since it is altogether inclined to assimilate even the concept of the mode of production, let us not hesitate to say that the mercantile mode of production or the mode of mercantile production well and truly exists, and exists in bourgeois ideology, for it exists only there. Better: it should be added that the mode of mercantile production is, for bourgeois ideology, the one and only existing mode of production, in the strong sense of the word existing, that is, the only one that deserves to exist, for it is in conformity with nature – with the nature of things and with human nature, which, as natures, are bedfellows in the big natural bed of the mode of mercantile production.

Let us observe, as discreetly as possible, how things happen there. What does the nature of things want and what does human nature want? It wants man to cultivate the land; it wants him to fence it round (Locke, Rousseau, Smith) and to produce enough to live on on it – enough for himself, his winsome wife and his enchanting children. Man is by nature a petty producer who cultivates nature and nature amply rewards his efforts, producing, as a result of his labour, enough to feed him – him and his little family. For the family is as natural as all the rest, is it not? But what happens? For man is such-and-such an individual, Pierre, Jean, Jacques; he tranquilly cultivates his plot in his neck of the woods. Alongside him is another Jean, Pierre or Paul who does the same thing. For, after all, the human race is made up of individuals – that is its nature, is it not? All these folks work, but as their imaginations do too, Pierre says to himself one fine day: 'But if I were to come to an agreement with my neighbour Paul to give him my surplus apples in exchange for his surplus pears?' Since the imagination is, as everyone knows, 'contagious' ('the contagious communications of strong imaginations', Malebranche),[56] this discovery spreads like wildfire, and soon all our independent petty producers with families set about becoming traders, that is, merchants.

One more step in the imagination and they invent money for us, which, as everybody knows, is made (by nature) to facilitate exchange: and, with that, trade gets underway. Our independent petty producers with families have become petty mercantile [*marchands*] producers: since the market is the natural consequence of the existence of merchants [*marchands*] (how powerful nature can be!), they bring their surplus production, whatever they don't consume themselves, to market. Nothing but what is natural in all this: nature produces everything, the producer who produces to satisfy his natural needs, including the natural needs of the woman whom he has taken to wife to satisfy his natural needs, and those of the children whom she has borne him, that is, whom he has begotten upon her to satisfy the human race's natural need to reproduce itself; the surplus yielded by a healthy natural activity rewarded by nature; the idea of trading surpluses, which satisfies a natural need; and the market which emerges naturally from the existence of petty producers who trade their surpluses. Presto! *The mercantile mode of production*: independent petty producers producing in order to sell (part of what they produce).

Taking one more step, one can imagine that, naturally, and above all after naturally shifting from agriculture to the production of manufactured objects once they have become artisans, these worthies naturally go to work producing exclusively in order to sell. You're not, after all, going to take it into your heads that a petty producer of shoes sells only the *surplus* of the shoes he has made, the ones he doesn't need! For everyone knows that the 'most poorly shod shoemaker', even if he is well shod, keeps just one pair a year for himself and three for the wife and kids, all the rest going to market. He produces in order to sell.

Thus it is that the capitalist is born. He is, at the outset, an independent petty producer who, thanks to his labour and his merits and his moral virtues, has succeeded in producing enough to sell enough to buy a few more tools, just what it takes to employ a few unfortunates who don't have anything to eat, because there's no room left on earth (which is 'round', that is, finite, limited, as Kant magnificently puts it)[57] and because they weren't able to become independent petty producers; he renders them the magnanimous service of giving them wages in exchange for their work. What generosity! But generosity too is in human nature. The fact that all this goes sour later, that the wage-workers have the bad grace to find that the work-day is too long and that their wages are too short, is also in human nature, which has its bad sides, just as it is in human nature that certain capitalistic independent petty producers take unfair advantage (evil sorts that they are!) of their wage-workers or, still worse, play tricks in their fashion, dirty tricks, on the other independent petty producers whom they regard (just imagine!) as their 'competitors' and treat mercilessly on the market. These things ought not to exist, but there are not only good people in this world: one has to bear the cross of human wickedness or thoughtlessness. For if they only knew!

If they knew, they would know what we have just said: that there exists one natural mode of production and just one, the mercantile mode of production, constituted by independent petty producers with families, who produce in order to sell either their surplus or everything they produce, working alone with their little family or employing wretches without house or home whom they provide, out of love for their fellow man, with the bread of a wage, thus becoming, quite naturally, capitalists, who can get bigger, if the God of Calvin, who rewards good works, bestows that grace on them.

Thus it is that the mercantile mode of production or the mode of mercantile production – based on the existence of independent petty producers who started out as subsistence farmers but were naturally destined to become merchants, part-time and then full-time merchants, and then merchants relying on wage-based (capitalist) production – is, for bourgeois ideology, *the only mode of production there is.*

There is no other. The others are just deviations or aberrations, conceived on the basis of this one and only mode: aberrations due to the fact that the Enlightenment had not penetrated people's minds with its self-evident truths in these times of darkness and obscurantism. This explains the scandalous horror of slavery: people did not know at the time that all men are free (= have a right to human nature = can be independent petty producers). This explains the horror of feudalism: people did not know at the time that the feudal independent petty producer, the serf, was capable of leaving his land, taking up residence elsewhere and trading his products for other products, like every man on earth – instead of remaining confined to the horrid closed circle of bare subsistence, merely attenuated by that other horror, the corvée for the lord and tithe for the Church.

If the mercantile mode of production is, for bourgeois ideology, the only mode of production in the world – all others being simply aberrations or deviations from it – the reason is that it fulfils the function of *founding* the capitalist mode of production as the only mode of production in the world. For what is the capitalist mode of production? (We continue to assume here that bourgeois ideology has consented to use the concept of mode of production, something it can perfectly well do: it has done all sorts of other things!) The capitalist mode of production is just the mercantile mode of production in its developed form, its naturally developed form: the mercantile mode of production serves to found the capitalist mode of production in bourgeois ideology, inasmuch as bourgeois ideology thinks the capitalist mode of production by way of the founding categories of the mercantile mode of production. Since the mercantile mode of production is perfectly mythical, an invention of the ideological imaginary, and since the act of foundation depends on the same imaginary, we have, on the one hand, the fact of the existence of the capitalist mode of production, which is terribly real, and, on the other, its theory, its essence, furnished us by the mythical, founding construction of the mercantile mode of production. The result of this act of imaginary foundation is as follows.

1. The capitalist mode of production, which exists, is the only one that can exist, the only one that exists, the only one that has a right to existence. The fact that it has not always existed (and even that must be qualified, for when we look into the matter in detail, we always find this reality, which is natural, everywhere: independent

petty producers), or that it has not always visibly existed, obscured as it was by horrid realities – this is merely an accident of history. It should have existed from all eternity and, thank God, it exists today, having carried the day against obscurantism, and we may be sure that nature having finally vanquished non-nature, light having finally triumphed over darkness, nature and light, that is, the capitalist mode of production, can be sure of existing for all eternity. It has finally been *recognized*!

2. This guarantee having been obtained at last, the essence having at last attained to existence, we can, at last, understand everything. If we want to understand what the capitalist mode of production is, it is enough to go have a look at its origin, that is, its essence, the mercantile mode of production: we will find men, the independent petty producers, their families and all the tra-la-la.

3. We have at last arrived at existence and since what has arrived at existence is the essence, we have everything we need: existence, murmuring with satisfaction, and the essence that allows us to understand it. That way everyone is happy.

That way, in other words, bourgeois ideology has reached its goal: representing the capitalist mode of production as the development of an imaginary mercantile mode of production, and the 'genesis' of the capitalist mode of production as the result of the work of deserving independent petty producers who became capitalists only because they really deserved to. It remains only to strike up the universal anthem of humanity's gratitude to free enterprise.[58]

This is what interests us about the matter. For this system of notions has weighed very heavily indeed on Marxist theory, and with good reason: all classical political economy is saturated with it, is merely a learned commentary on it. It has effects in Marx himself, although he had everything he needed to guard himself against these dangers, but above all in the Marxists whom even Marx is not sufficient to protect against this contagion (when they do not read him, obviously, but even when they do).

It is, however, necessary to form a clear idea of these pseudo-difficulties; and it is rather easy to do so.

When Marx talks about *mercantile production*, this term by no means implies the existence of a pseudo-mode of mercantile production. What is mercantile production? It is that part of production which is either marketed [*commercialisé*] as a surplus or produced to be marketed. No less, but no more. In all modes of production in which mercantile relations exist, there is mercantile production. For it is not possible for mercantile relations, market relations, to exist unless there is production that is exchanged for the general equivalent, money, on the market. This production is called mercantile production because it proceeds by way of the mercantile relations of mercantile circulation. And that is all.

However, as I have already said, mercantile production can be represented by the surplus of non-mercantile production or, on the contrary, can result from purely mercantile production, production carried out to be sold. Production of the latter sort can be *localized* in a mode of production (this holds for all pre-capitalist modes of production in which mercantile relations exist), that is, can exist 'in its pores', as Marx says.[59] It can, on the contrary, be generalized, as it is in the capitalist mode of production. That, however, changes nothing about this business: in no case, not even in the capitalist mode of production, does mercantile production stem from a supposed mercantile mode of production. I think this is now clear enough, no?

What is apparently more complicated is the question of the 'independent petty producers', on which all the bourgeois ideology of society, history and political economy rests. It is all the more complicated in that Marx often talks about 'independent petty producers', in terms that are not always clear.

It must even be admitted that Marx did not entirely manage to rid himself, in all of his texts (I say 'in all of his texts' because, in many texts, he did manage to), of the idea that the independent petty producer is in some sense a '*natural*' reality. Marx thereby endorses, willy-nilly, an essential category of bourgeois ideology, the category of 'nature', which is quite simply intended to found existing fact in its origin in right [*origine de droit*]. (Nature is that which possesses right [*droit*], and this is why all 'natural law' [*droit naturel*] jurists talk, precisely, about 'natural law': nature is what is *rightful* [*de droit*], a notion that brooks no appeal in a period in which Right is the highest bourgeois authority over the bourgeois fact of the capitalist relation of production.) Similarly, the monogamous family (wife and children) seems 'natural' as a unit of production and consumption. Similarly, it seems 'natural' that the independent petty producer should live in a monogamous family, begin to trade his surplus and, if he is meritorious enough to have accumulated the where-withal to employ wage-workers, become a capitalist. He is the *homo (individuum) oeconomicus* in originary form.

However, it is not just bourgeois ideology which impresses Marx, it is also something completely different: *the real existence of independent petty producers*, roughly corresponding to the figure of the independent petty producer as presented by bourgeois ideology, throughout a lengthy period running from the late Middle Ages to the contemporary period. These independent petty producers are the ones who were expropriated during the sinister history of primitive accumulation.[60] They are the ones we find again, paradoxically, in certain Western countries such as France (whereas they were decimated in Great Britain) and, in our own day, we still find them in France (the owners of family farms). An attempt is underway to establish them in 'underdeveloped' countries in order to 'accelerate' these countries' 'development' (Africa) and so on.[61] They are the ones who were eliminated by the collectivization of the land in the USSR under Stalin and so on. In short, a reality that resists.

To take just this one example, when Marx lambastes the bourgeois theory of the origin of capitalism (in the independent petty producer), opposing his theory of primitive accumulation to it, he encounters, precisely, independent petty producers not as the origin of capitalism, but as that which capitalism had to do away with in order to establish itself on the ruins of the feudal mode of production.[62] So, plainly, independent petty producers really exist! And if that is not related to a so-called mercantile mode of production, what is it?

If the reader here recalls what was said of the feudal mode of production, I believe I can advance the hypothesis that, at least in the case of the capitalist Europe that emerged from feudalism, the independent petty producer, far from being, as bourgeois ideology believes, the originary form of the capitalist mode of production, is an organic form of the feudal mode of production. For the independent petty producer assisted by his family (a unit of production and a unit of consumption) possesses his means of production and his labour-power. We have seen that, in the feudal mode of production, he possesses them 'relatively' (this is equivalent to relative 'non-possession'), because the land to which he is bound is in the lord's 'eminent domain' and because his labour-power does not really belong to him, since, first, it is bound to the land, which the serf cannot leave and since, second, it is at the lord's disposal (work on the lord's land, corvées and so on).

Under the feudal mode of production, these features are visible and pertinent enough to make further explanation superfluous. When, however, this *form* of the feudal relation of production survives under other conditions, maintaining itself even under the conditions of the capitalist mode of production, one hesitates to identify it as typical of the feudal relation of production. For it does in fact exist under another mode of production that has now become dominant and this alters some of its features.

It will be objected that the same holds for ground rent. Something in this comparison is on the mark. I believe, however, that we can defend the idea that the form of 'independent petty production' is not as deeply penetrated by the capitalist relation of production as ground rent is.

For if the petty producer is no longer legally bound to his land the way the serf was, he is bound to it practically. He is bound to it by 'laws' other than those of serfdom (his debts and so on), but the fact is that there are no migrations of peasant petty producers. They remain on their land: it holds them fast. Of course, [the petty producer] is no longer subject to the corvée and disposes 'freely' of his labour-power, but he is 'bound' by ties that are just as strong, those of an indebtedness which he never manages to overcome and so on.

That, however, is not the most important point. What subsists *intact* from the feudal mode of production is not just the fact of bare self-sufficiency (which is quite secondary here), but the relation of the direct producer known as the independent petty producer to his own labour-power and that of his family. And this relation, right in the middle of the capitalist regime, in which wage-labour reigns supreme, is a relation *that does not involve commodity relations*. All reconstructions undertaken by bourgeois or Marxist economists for the purpose of assessing the value of the labour-power invested in a family farm are fictive reconstructions that simply neglect *the fact* that this labour-power is a use-value which is not an exchange-value and, therefore, has no value. All attempts at quantification stumble over this little 'problem', which is in fact the index of a crucial reality: namely, that the independent petty producer, far from being the prototype of a capitalist, far from being a capitalist, is a 'foreign body' in the capitalist mode of production, quite simply because he represents a form inherited from the feudal mode of production that has resisted history and evolution.

This is a point that cannot be emphasized too strongly. For the idea that the independent petty producer is virtually a capitalist (a little one can become a big one, and the big one will be a capitalist), and the (*still graver*) idea that nothing is more 'natural' than the independent petty producer – these ideas are so deeply rooted among our everyday self-evident truths, they are so closely bound up with centuries of bourgeois ideology, that we must at all costs analyse and explain them in order to unmask them as bourgeois myths, as the bourgeois myth par excellence.

It isn't true. Independent petty production (in the case of peasants and artisans alike) has nothing 'natural' about it (no more than does the monogamous family that serves as its base and furnishes it with its workforce): it is the result of a process constituted at an identifiable time in our French history, namely, under the feudal mode of production. It isn't true: independent petty production (even if certain petty producers, after becoming big ones, are transformed into capitalists) has nothing to do with capitalist forms of production and is not latently [*virtuellement*] capitalistic.

I said that, for us, the independent petty producer harks back to the feudal mode of production. At least for us in Western Europe and, at any rate, in England and France as well as in Italy. Why this reservation? Because we cannot rule out the possibility that the form 'independent petty producer' can exist on the basis of modes of production other than the feudal mode of production: in Greece and Rome, for example, hence in the slave-based mode of production. In these cases, however, one would have to [know] (this is beyond my competency) the specific conditions of existence of these forms, which history has at all events eradicated, for, to the best of my knowledge, these independent petty producers disappeared, in their Roman form, in the face of the big slave-holders with big landholdings, to be resurrected in the form of serfs under medieval feudalism.

The important point therefore seems to me to be the following.

There exists a form that may be termed 'independent petty production', understood in the sense we have defined: the independent petty producer with his family, using his labour-power and that of his family to mobilize his means of production (with partial non-possession or partial possession).

There is nothing natural about this form. (What is more, every expression in which the term 'natural' figures should be struck from theoretical existence. Nothing is less 'natural', for example, than the 'economy' which is said to be 'natural'. Nothing is less 'natural' than such-and-such a form of kinship relations, hence of family relations.)

This form can exist in different modes of production, doubtless with variations in its features (which call for study), but with constant elements as well.

When this form exists in a mode of production, it is either characteristic of that mode of production (as in the feudal mode of production) or it is atypical for that mode of production and harks back to the form characteristic of another mode of production (for example, the form 'independent petty production' in the capitalist mode of production) or, again, it is a secondary form, a 'sub-form', a 'transformed form' of the mode of production under consideration (this may be the case in the slave-based mode of production in Greece and Rome). (In this last case, see whether it is not a product of mercantile relations, one of the products of mercantile relations.)

Since this form is not *natural*, it cannot be arbitrarily imposed on an existing mode of production to facilitate or accelerate its development. Here an incredible number of problems and difficulties converge; they are, unfortunately, not just theoretical, but political and historical as well.

Consider Marx's experience, Marx's double experience. In [1853] he wrote on India and predicted that the development of capitalism there would lead to the disintegration of Hindu society, imposing 'classic' capitalist forms on it (the petty Hindu peasant was going to become an independent petty producer: commodity relations would impose this).[63] Then, ten years later, Marx admitted that he had been mistaken and that the existing relations of production in India had shown an amazing capacity to resist 'the new forms'.[64] Strange. ... What new forms? In any case, India has pursued its history, which presents the little disadvantage of not adhering to the evolutionary scheme of the 'natural' succession of the obligatory modes of production. ... Might this mean that there exist forms that refuse to fall into line?

Marx, however, wrote at the end of his life (to Vera Zasulich) about the *mir* in order to consider the possibility that *other forms* (other than independent petty production, supposedly imposed by the capitalist mode of production) could be envisaged for the transition to socialism. The ('natural') Russian peasant community would do just as well, under certain conditions. In any case, this is a question it would be a mistake to neglect.[65]

Did Lenin and the Bolsheviks neglect it? The fact is that, for obvious political reasons, they had to proclaim that the land was to be divided up: the land to the tiller. The land to the tiller, by all means. But does this mean that it had to be divided up? Was it necessary, in other words, to create a multitude of tens of millions of independent petty producers? The history of the Russian revolution is too chaotic for us to be able to understand it clearly already. Yet the fact is that, amid the dire poverty that followed the war, and during the war of foreign intervention and the civil war, the unfortunate peasants, lacking tools for production and, perhaps, the training required to engage in individual production of this kind, had, for various reasons, to resort to selling their plots to bigger peasants, who grew proportionally still bigger and came to constitute the stratum of the kulaks. We should ask ourselves whether Lenin, although he had drawn interesting conclusions about 'the development of capitalism in Russia (in the countryside)' from the statistics of the *zemstvos*,[66] did not generalize his conclusions too hastily, neglecting that which was not capitalistic in the countryside, and also assuming rather too hastily, because he was extrapolating from conclusions that Kautsky had drawn from Marx (*The Agrarian Question*),[67] that the order of Western succession was mandatory in all countries, thus underestimating the non-capitalistic elements.

If this extremely hazardous hypothesis has some truth to it, we would find, here, a whiff of the evolutionism that accompanies the 'natural' bourgeois theory of the mercantile mode of production and the independent petty producer as latently [*virtuellement*] capitalistic. If we go to the heart of the question, we shall be forced to ask ourselves whether the Marxist theory of both capitalist ground rent and the 'agrarian question' has not too quickly aligned the countryside with the cities, and the 'normal' course of agrarian development with the 'normal' course of urban development. Yet Marx (in a merely allusive way, it is true; but this is a thesis altogether essential to Marxism) had clearly said and shown that the opposition or difference between town and country (which communism must abolish) is an organic feature of the capitalist mode of production, and that the capitalist mode of production irremediably accentuates this difference.[68]

If words mean something, what does that mean? It means that there is a basic inequality in development between the cities and the countryside from the viewpoint of the capitalist mode of production, as a function of the capitalist relation of production. But, if so, why this lag and what are its effects? Productivity is higher in the cities (industry). Yet the capitalist mode of production originated in the countryside! (The enclosures and, in France, the Physiocrats.) What are we to conclude? What, if not the continued existence, in the countryside, of feudal forms that have 'resisted' better than in the cities (as they resisted in India)? But if the forms of the feudal mode of production subsist more easily and [are better] capable of resisting in the countryside than in the city, the question, again, is why?

This is a question that merits very serious attention. It can shed light on what we said above (every social formation is 'in transit' between two modes of production, with elements of the preceding mode ...), from which we may derive the idea that we must, each time, look very closely at what happens in a social formation of a given mode of production and abandon the notion that that mode of production is realized *in pure form* in the social formation. This is a *political* question of the very first importance, since it commands the measures to be taken in the countryside (and elsewhere, but above all in the countryside, the 'black spot' in the policy of the socialist countries, China excepted, and, perhaps, the 'black spot' in Marxist theory).

Let us conclude that there is no mercantile mode of production; that there exist independent petty producers; but that, since their existence is not 'natural', despite the seeming identity of their form, what matters is to know the mode of production to which they belong when they figure in a given social formation, in order to be able to treat them accordingly and to know that we cannot impose their form on any social formation we like.

12. What has been said of the relation of production that defines a mode of production allows us to go back to the question of the pseudo-mode of socialist production.

Socialism is ordinarily defined by 1. collective ownership of the means of production, and 2. working-class power. Since the second characteristic concerns the superstructure, it is not relevant to a definition of the supposed relation of production in question. We are left with the first characteristic.

Let us recall that the relation of production of a mode of production is defined by the relation between the direct producers on the one hand and the productive forces (means of production and labour-power) on the other.

In the socialist social formation, we observe the following:

Labour-power continues to pass by way of the relative possession of the wage form, a commodity form. At the legal level, nothing about the relation of production of the capitalist mode of production has changed, in principle.

As for the means of production, the direct producers possess them not directly, but indirectly, by way of 'collective property' (the state, production co-operatives).

Thus, we are here still in the form of non-possession (the wage form) of labour-power, accompanied by non-possession of the means of production, corrected, however, by indirect possession.

This is what allows us to say that Lenin's formula is accurate: in the socialist social formation there co-exist, in contradictory fashion, elements belonging to the capitalist relation of production and elements preparing the communist relation of production.

The latter is prepared by collective ownership of the means of production and by a whole series of arrangements: the plan, guarantees that control the labour market, a wage structure that tends to reduce wage differentials and, generally speaking, organizational measures that tend to prepare communal forms of the management of enterprises and of the nation (measures that aim to attenuate and then do away with the division of labour, the division between mental and manual labour, the division between town and country and so on).

Everything turns on the political effort to reduce the elements that depend on the capitalist relation of production and develop the elements that prepare the communist mode of production. Everything turns on that, for the outcome has not been decided in advance. Mistakes can compromise everything, making the tendency swing in the other direction. (A point that is misunderstood: the town-and-country division, which brings us back to the questions raised above. Marx's comment on this question has not really been taken seriously. Yet it is decisive. Capitalism took things as it found them: immense stretches of countryside and a handful of cities – and, after an initial period of vacillation, in which it established itself in the country, it developed frenetically in the cities, monstrously intensifying the unequal development of cities and countryside to the cities' advantage. This too seems 'natural'. It is taken for granted that cities are the factories' place of predilection. Why? Means of communication, population density? The endpoint of all the trade routes bringing raw materials? Yet one should be aware, after all, that in the seventeenth and eighteenth centuries, much of industry developed *in the countryside*, near rivers and mines. Thus there is nothing 'natural' about the development of the cities.

We should find out the reasons for this, reasons that have perhaps already been discovered, although I do not know them. Perhaps what has been called commercial capitalism, which spread from the ports (consider Venice, The Hague, London, Bordeaux and so on) to continental cities? Perhaps political reasons as well? However that may be, the development of the cities to the detriment of the countryside bears the mark of the capitalist economy and capitalist politics, perhaps even that of the capitalist class struggle. (Did capitalism escape, in the cities, the landed aristocracy, its enemy at the time?)

In this regard, the policies of Stalin and of the contemporary USSR bear the same mark. Chinese policy, in contrast, is headed in the direction Marx thought desirable. Stalin's policy went hand in hand with his policy of socialist accumulation at the peasants' expense. This was another negative consequence of the 1917 revolution's bad agrarian policy (bad ... it is hard to affirm this in perfectly cut-and-dried fashion).

[The Main Contradiction][69]

1. The main contradiction

The thesis with which the Resolution of the Eighty and other resolutions begin, the contradiction between 'the imperialist camp' and 'the socialist camp', should be refuted.[70]

This contradiction is not antagonistic, and it has not even been, since the end of the Cold War (the reasons for the end of the Cold War have to be closely re-examined) – it has not *only* been the strength of the 'socialist camp' and the peoples struggling for their liberation + the international working class which have succeeded in bringing about the end of the 'Cold War', but also imperialist reasons specific to imperialism, to its visions of gaining a foothold in certain socialist countries financially – new Marshall Plans, this time for the direct use of certain socialist countries: economically (the effect of loans) and politically, among other means, by utilizing the effects of the split in the international Communist movement, and exacerbating it. Under these novel conditions, the USA no longer needs a policy of military 'rollback'. The policy of financial imperialism + the contradictions between the USSR and China serve its ends much better, clearing the way for a policy of 'peaceful co-existence' followed by economic 'co-operation'(!).

The main contradiction is the antagonistic contradiction between the capitalist class on the global scale and the working class on the global scale + the allies of the global working class, namely, the peoples struggling for their liberation.

This contradiction is antagonistic. It can find a solution (as the phrase goes) only by abolishing one of its terms, the capitalist class of the imperialist countries – only by ending imperialism.

Naturally, it is a question of an antagonistic contradiction here – but one that can be 'treated' in non-antagonistic fashion, if the struggle of the working class is opportunistic. If, for example, the USSR opens its doors to a new Marshall Plan, which it has even requested (of the USA and the FRG [Federal Republic of Germany, or West Germany], and soon of Japan as well)! This economic 'opening' is not just economic. It has political effects that shape the foreign 'policy' and therefore also the domestic 'policy' of the communist parties in the imperialist countries. If the working class does not manage to break this 'circle', it may find itself waiting quite some time for the 'fall', that is, the end of imperialism. Even in this case, however, it is foreseeable that the facts of the crisis (monetary and soon, economic, and ultimately, political) will educate, in their hard school, working-class militants, and that these militants will enter into the dance at a rhythm altogether different from the one that the party leaderships impose on them.

2. The contemporary crisis of the international communist movement should be considered in the light of this main contradiction.

Apparently, we are in a crisis from which there is no exit. Apparently. But this is not the first time. In 1914, how many militants in Europe believed that, three years later, a revolution could break out somewhere in the world, and triumph? One could count them on the fingers of two hands after the 'treason of the Second International': the 'social-chauvinist' political line of all the leaders of the socialist and social-democratic parties.

In 1914, Lenin was practically alone, with a few friends. In 1917, at the time of the April theses, he would be alone before all the leaders of the CP(b) who had come to welcome him at the train station in Saint-Petersburg – although, by this time, the revolution had broken out in Russia!

[The Illusion of Competition, the Reality of War]

Hypothesis (to be verified): the capitalist relation of production is such that it implies

1. exploitation, and thus class struggle (class struggle on both sides, but first, so to speak, on that of the capitalist class); and

2. the 'play' of the capitalist mode of production within its own 'limits', which are absolute: it cannot get beyond them by itself.

The consequence would seem to be that the depiction of competition as a *cause* of 1. concentration and 2. the growth of capital (to withstand competition: a theory of preventive warfare, in sum, preventive economic warfare, where everything transpires between capitalists alone, in line with the Spinozist metaphor about the fish, which has it that the big ones eat the little ones, growing fat on the little ones,[71] which gives us a theory wholly predicated on the competition between capitalists, while, at the same time, workers are condemned to compete with each other until they form associations) – the consequence would seem to be that this theory is a bourgeois theory.

The consequence would likewise seem to be that the depiction of the first phase of capitalism as that of '*competitive*' capitalism is itself either purely descriptive, since it talks about an effect (but this should be said), or wrong.

It would follow that the truth is to be sought elsewhere.

Marx says so, repeatedly, in connection with the tendency of the rate of profit to fall: competition does not cause the fall in the profit rate, but, quite the contrary, the fall in the profit rate causes competition. The economic Darwinism of competition (which once again harks back to the bourgeois-ideological image of the independent petty producer struggling against the others) is wrong.

Competition is an 'illusion' (Marx).[72]

Where, then, should we look for the cause of both competition and other effects attributable to competition (such as concentration)? We should look for it, precisely, in the tendency of the rate of profit to fall, in what it conceals and shows: namely, the class struggle.

Where does the fall in the rate of profit come from? From the increase in the proportion c/v,[73] that is, from the development of productivity, that is, from the partial, tendential replacement of absolute surplus value by relative surplus value. But this 'displacement' is, *in its very principle*, an effect of the class struggle.

(The false representations:

1. The desire for gain (psychology).

2. Negating this psychology: the law of competition (described by Hobbes) or the State of War.

3. The law of this State of War: preventive warfare. All competition is preventive. The 'free' psychology of the man who 'wants to enrich himself' or 'seeks gain' is nothing but the movement[74] of an unconscious law: play the game or die. The Law of the State of War.

Bourgeois theory fails to get beyond it.

Hobbes's 'desire for gain', or 'competition', can be sublimated in the *'point d'honneur'* represented by the quest for 'glory', which Hegel was to transform into 'self-recognition', the 'desire to be desired', the 'desire to be recognized' (with, naturally, death as its terminus).)

The hypothesis/theory about competition stated above obviously presupposes that one has 'settled scores' with a preliminary question of crucial importance: that of the establishment of a mode of production – in the case to hand, the capitalist mode of production.

It presupposes

1. that we have a certain idea of what it means to exist for a mode of production: the conditions of its existence – of its enduring reproduction – and of the relationship of this existence to non-existence. In other words, it presupposes that we have a clear understanding of the fact that a mode of production may not exist, may exist and perish as soon as it appears or, on the contrary, may grow stronger and pursue its historical destiny. This presupposes a theory of the conditions of existence that is at the same time a theory of the conditions of the non-existence or disappearance of a mode of production. For we always reason on the basis of accomplished fact and nothing else. How did this fact come to be accomplished? Everything is there. Although the capitalist mode of production has already died several times before subsisting as we know

it, before 'taking' on the feudal mode of production or on others;

2. that we have rejected, once and for all, the theory of independent petty producers as the origin of capitalism. They are feudal, not capitalist, petty producers. Capitalism came from elsewhere: from the 'owners of money' (Marx). For then we very easily succumb to the illusion of believing that these independent petty producers are 'naturally' (according to the good old bourgeois ideology of capitalism) 'competitors' in an idyllic marketplace;

3. that we have assimilated what Marx says several times in *Capital* – this is in fact the theory of recognition of the accomplished fact – namely, that the capitalist mode of production itself creates its own basis, that is to say, reproduces itself = exists.[75] (Find these texts of Marx's and interpret them to mean self-reproduction = existence.)

When the capitalist mode of production exists, it 'functions' in the way Marx's analysis indicates, in accordance with the fall in the rate of profit (that is, the economic effect of the class struggle). Competition is then just a subordinate effect, a cause-effect, to be sure, yet a subordinate effect.

In the emergence of a mode of production such as the capitalist mode of production, we can always ask: But then why, but then how did it emerge? And we always fall back on the same bourgeois nonsense (work and so on). If we get beyond it, however, we are pretty ill-at-ease. Why did *this* mode of production emerge? Why wage-labour?

To this, we can give Marx's answer: the encounter of the owners of money, hence of an accumulation capable of functioning formally as capital, on the one hand, and 'free labourers' on the other.[76] In a certain way, this is enough to answer the question, starting out from the observation that this encounter produced the accomplished fact of existing capitalism, that is to say, self-reproducing capitalism.

Behind this explanation, however, there is another accomplished fact: namely, that the waged relation of production is the solution to the 'crisis' of the serf-based relation of production at the heart of an exploitative society. In sum, a relation of exploitation is substituted for a relation of exploitation as the solution to its historic 'crisis'. These gentlemen never get beyond relations of exploitation. The proof is the 'good' English revolution: friends, all friends, old-style exploiters and new-style exploiters alike.

Hence the idea that the transition to communism can in no case represent a solution to the 'crisis' of the capitalist relation of production. For a good reason: capitalist 'crises' resolve themselves all by themselves (in the form of imperialist wars, among other ways) or produce, like good chickens at the end of their wits, the 'ducks' known as proletarian revolutions![77]

When the Party says that the Common Programme[78] offers a solution to the 'crisis of state monopoly capitalism', it is either telling the truth, in which case this is a bourgeois programme, or else it should say that the Common Programme offers the workers prospects not of resolving the capitalist regime's crisis, but of exiting from that regime by putting an end to it. One can find the words to say that, even in taking the much ballyhooed 'transition' into account (new democracy).[79]

* * *

Give yourself, for starters, a capitalist honest enough to answer your questions and admit that he is driven to increase his fortune indefinitely, without pause and without respite. Ask him *why* he yields to this irresistible tendency. You will receive, in this order (disorder would be another order, the same order) the following answers:

1. The *psychological* capitalist will tell you: 'I'm greedy and bent on acquiring wealth. My nature is such that I thirst for gold and my thirst is such that it makes me thirsty even when it's slaked. Everyone knows the story about the sea: Why doesn't it overflow? Answer: Because there is a goodly number of fish in the sea, and they drink a tremendous amount of water; since the water's salty, they're always thirsty. We can only conclude that gold too is salty, since it makes a man thirsty all the time (thirsty for gold). Enough joking. Psychology, which always keeps

philosophy and religion in the corner of its eye, answers: it's in the nature of things and in human nature too; man is a creature of desire and is therefore insatiable, for desire is infinite. Whatever the world contains in the way of philosophers knows this, from Aristotle talking about chrematistics[80] down to Pascal and countless others: it is because man is finite that he is condemned to desire's 'bad infinity' (Hegel).[81] There you have the reason that the capitalist enriches himself without end, to the point of losing sleep and desire – human nature's to blame.

2. The *philosophical* capitalist (a notch more sophisticated), versed in Hobbes and Hegel, will tell you: but my dear fellow, nature only reveals itself in its 'sublation'! This desire that you think you bring to bear on mere *things*, such as goods, wealth or power (power is merely a means of procuring goods, or the men who procure goods) reaches infinitely higher! For example, if so-and-so chases after gold, it is less to satisfy a need (or desire) for wealth or power (for in these matters everything has its limits, and if man's desire is infinite, man isn't) than because he is seeking an altogether different good: the esteem of his peers, that which Hobbes calls 'glory' and Hegel calls 'recognition'. Thus the race for wealth and the race for power (the means of attaining wealth) are merely the *obligatory* detour that a law takes in order to impose itself on human individuals. In fact, look! The rich man always enriches himself at another man's expense; the powerful man always becomes powerful at a third party's expense. Universal competition rules the world and men are merely its puppets. Not competition for property and power: no, whoa! Competition is a more mysterious, more sophisticated desire: the desire for glory and recognition. Man wants only to be esteemed and recognized for what he is: more deserving than the others (Hobbes) or simply free (Hegel), by way of the figures of the master and slave. Thus, competition for goods and power is simply the means of, and a pretext for, competition of another kind, in which every man expects recognition of his 'glory' or 'freedom' from those he dominates. The insatiable thirst for riches thereby becomes an altogether spiritual affair,

in which man can stand tall and proud for being endowed with a nature so dignified that it puts him a hundred feet above the base passions that were attributed to him. One may well be a bourgeois, one still has one's sense of honour.

3. The *realistic* capitalist (a notch more sophisticated theoretically), better versed in Hobbes, will tell you: The quest for 'glory' is one thing! What matters is something else: the law that forces all men to seek glory, without sparing a one. For how is it that men are brought to engage in this frantic quest, by what power? To be sure, they all start out by desiring goods and, later, glory; but the fact that they *all* desire them with so equal a desire that this desire surpasses and governs them, and the fact that they are all, without exception, enrolled in the race – that is what calls for explanation. The reason is that, when the time comes, they unleash, unawares, the power of a law that annuls its origin: universal war, the war of all against all. The whole mystery of the matter resides in this conversion: individuals desiring goods, each for [his own] petty ends, and suddenly all of them together are thrown into a war so universal that it becomes a State of War. That is, a State of relations such that the war can flare up at any moment and anywhere (it's like bad weather, Hobbes writes: it doesn't rain every day or everywhere, but it *could* rain any time, anywhere at all) should someone attack someone else.[82] With the establishment of this State of Universal Competition, aptly called the State of War and a War of all against all, that is to say, a war of the first person who happens along against the second, things are converted a second time. Fear of being attacked makes men make the first move and war reveals itself for what it is: the essence of war is to be *preventive*.

With that, the portrait of competition is complete.

Let us lay our cards on the table.

Bourgeois ideology can come up with a 'psychological' explanation of the 'valorization of value', of the capitalist's 'frantic quest for profits'. This explanation doesn't go very far, for the much vaunted 'human nature' that serves as its warrant admits of – what a coincidence! – strange exceptions: those of the known modes of production in which this frantic quest for profits is absent (in classless societies and those parts of modes of production untouched by commodity relations).

Bourgeois ideology can also afford itself the luxury of 'sublimating' material competition between capitalists in a philosophical theory of recognition of the self.

However, this theory always ends up lapsing back into that which serves as its ground: a theory of the State of War or of Competition. At that point, the iron law of competition makes its entry onto the scene and governs the competing individuals. Yet this straightforward theory does not go very far either. For if it acknowledges that a necessity presides over the conflicts of competition, this necessity is never anything other than the concept of the universality of conflicts and of their immediate inversion: from defence to attack by way of *prevention*.

That is, nevertheless, how one might be tempted to explain, but in the bourgeois mode, the capitalist tendency to accumulate or, again, the capitalist tendency to intensify exploitation. It will be said, for example, that this irresistible tendency is engendered by competition between capitalists. So-and-so, who exploits his workers and encounters his adversaries in, simultaneously, the market for means of production, the market for labour and the market for commodities, will, because he is fearful of disappearing as a result of the others' competition, very naturally begin, *preventively*, to exploit his workers even more, so as to be sufficiently strong later on, when adversity strikes. And as everyone else does the same thing, there is no reason for the whirligig ever to stop turning. What results is what we in fact observe: the tendency to extract a maximum of surplus value and to keep on lengthening the working-day, to keep on intensifying labour (augmenting productivity) and to keep on accumulating in the capitalist mode (in order to extract more and more surplus value). And we will imagine that we have gone to the bottom of things and come up with the reason for this strange tendency.

However, when we take a closer look at this preventive war that the capitalists wage on each other, it turns out to be a singular war! It pits the combatants against each other, of course, like every war, even the war of all against all. But the combatants, that is, the capitalists, do not really confront each other, since they spend their time protecting themselves against attack by taking preventive measures. In Hobbes's war, we might suppose that it is a question of real attacks and that the parties preventively carry out real attacks so as not to be attacked. The same holds here: but rather than preventively launching real attacks, one simply beefs up one's forces, preventively, so as not to fall. To be sure, there are victims, bankruptcies, people left by the wayside. Yet, overall, the capitalists as a group come off rather well, so much so that Marx says of competition that it is ordinarily their 'friendly society':[83] it is less the rule of the war they wage on each other than that of the war that they don't. Can we therefore say that this State of War is a State of Peace? My word, as far as the capitalist class as a whole is concerned, yes.

But then where is the war? Elsewhere: between the capitalists and their workers. By means of competition, the capitalist class adjusts its accounts rather than settling them – but behind competition, which Marx calls an 'illusion',[84] the capitalist class wages a veritable war on the working class. For, ultimately, taken at its word, this theory of preventive war shows that prevention, well conducted, spares the capitalists war against other capitalists; it shows that the working class bears the full brunt of prevention, that prevention of the pseudo-war between capitalists is a permanent war against the working class. In that, the war is not at all universal, a war of all against all, as Hobbes claims; it is a war of the capitalist class against the working class. Thus, the war that the capitalist class wages on the working class simply allows the capitalists to live in peace. We had been mixing up our wars. We had mistaken competition for a war. We had forgotten the class struggle.

We come now to the root of everything: a certain representation of capitalism's history, a *bourgeois* representation of capitalism's history.

I explained earlier how the myth that the 'independent petty producer' constitutes the consubstantial essence of capitalism and its origin haunts the bourgeois depiction of capitalism in its entirety. At the origins there were, we are told, individuals working for themselves with their means of production. With a certain degree of development of the productive forces, some of what they produce is commercialized (through an exchange of surpluses), resulting in an initial accumulation. The same independent petty producers, become wealthy traders, are then supposed to have offered unfortunates without house or home money (wages) in exchange for the strength of their arms to operate their means of production, thus becoming capitalists producing exclusively for the market. This continuous process naturally culminates (in this story, everything is natural) – beginning with mercantile production's first forms of existence and steadily intensifying with its expansion – in the competition of the petty mercantile producers becoming capitalists in different markets: the market for commodities, means of production and, finally, capital. The law of competition is thus supposed, in [some] sense, to have naturally 'taken over from' [*prendre le 'relai' de*] the natural law of labour, production and the profitable exchange of initial surpluses, in order to accelerate the course of things, eliminate the weak, make the strong stronger, intensify exploitation (but one prefers to hush that one up), precipitate concentration, bring monopolies into existence and so on. Shall we just say 'take over from'? The law of competition, on that hypothesis, [is merely] the law of independent petty mercantile production pursued by different means or, rather, in different forms – for what is more natural than this confrontation between real forces, from which their truth emerges?

Barbarism? Fascism was a Preliminary Form of It

What is imperialism? 'The highest stage of capitalism' (Lenin).

Everyone knows this formula. But, as Hegel says,

'well-known' things are the least well known, precisely because they are the most familiar.[85]

This formula of Lenin's is a case in point. What exactly does it mean?

There is a whole history behind it! When, in 1916, Lenin wrote his short pamphlet on imperialism (it is just a short pamphlet, nothing more, written hastily and on the basis of the only documents he had at his disposal, and written under censorship, hence in 'a slave's language'),[86] he called it 'Imperialism, the highest [*suprême*] stage of capitalism'.[87] '*Suprême*' is the translation of a Russian word that means 'the biggest, the highest', hence 'the culminating point'. This word is found in Lenin's manuscript. Thereafter, as is well known, Lenin had other things to do. And when Czarism was overthrown in 1917 and Kerensky's Mensheviks [took] power, it so happened that Lenin's little pamphlet was published. The worthy Mensheviks made a very slight alteration to the title: they replaced the Russian word that means 'the culminating point' with another Russian word that means 'the most recent', 'the last to date'. Thus, Lenin's pamphlet was published under the title 'Imperialism, the most recent stage of capitalism'.[88] A small but significant difference.

The most recent is not necessarily the last. It is just the most recent. Other stages of capitalism can come after the most recent stage, imperialism: they have their chance! With that, our worthy Mensheviks, playing politically on the adjective, marked their distance from poor Lenin, who, in treating imperialism as the culminating stage of capitalism, gave a subsequent stage no chance at all.

There, for example, is one very little thing that is not well known, yet speaks volumes.

For Lenin, there is no other stage of capitalism after imperialism. Imperialism is therefore the last stage, not the 'most recent'. The last, full-stop. This means that capitalism has a history; it began, developed, grew, and now here we are, we have arrived at its last stage, imperialism. Afterwards, it's over. It's all over for capitalism. What do we have then? Socialism, obviously.

Yes and no. For Lenin did not write that imperialism

was the 'last stage' of capitalism. He wrote that it was the 'culminating stage' (highest [*suprême*] is not a good translation). This certainly means, beyond a doubt, that imperialism is the last stage of capitalism, but it also means something more, something extremely interesting: it means that imperialism is the 'culminating' point of capitalism, hence that 'afterwards' there can only be degeneration, if imperialism lasts. Precisely what Lenin calls 'decay' or 'stagnation',[89] which is already inscribed in imperialism. For this 'culminating' stage is already the stage of 'decay', 'parasitism' and 'stagnation'.

This allows us to make 'afterwards' more precise. We should not picture the history of capitalism as a train trip: after passing through a series of stations (of stages), capitalism's train arrives at imperialism the way the Paris–Marseille train arrives at Saint Charles station. Last stop! All passengers are requested to leave the train. Or, to call a spade a spade, imperialism isn't the last stage of capitalism in the sense in which afterwards it's over, it's all over for capitalism – and then what do we have? Socialism. No. It's over, but it's not, for it can still last a long time. If we don't move on to socialism, the stagnation will intensify and the rot will spread. It may take frightful forms, of which the decay of certain modes of production in history (the 'decadence of Rome') offers a very vague idea. If we don't move on to socialism, we will have, in sum, 'barbarism'. When we examine Lenin's adjective closely, we find Engels's old formula again: 'socialism or barbarism'.[90] Yes, that is how things are, that is, imperialism is so constructed, that is, imperialism imposes a form on class struggle such that we are standing at the 'bifurcation', the 'crossroads': either the working class will succeed, by means of its class struggle, in imposing socialism, and we will set out on the Long March which, by way of the dictatorship of the proletariat, will lead to communism, or else it will fail (for a while or forever) and we will be doomed to 'barbarism', that is, the forms of decomposition and stagnation of imperialism itself.

Of course, this 'either-or' will not be decided right away. The working class has not yet arrived at socialism in so-and-so many countries, but our fate has not been sealed for all that. Even if the working class lost the initiative, it would still be able to take it back. Even if its combat has not yet reached the level of seizing state power, the immense mass movements underway throughout the world and in our country are reason to think that the working class has the strength to wage its combat until it wins. And we have every reason to believe that, even if we have to go through a certain period of the over-putrefaction [*sur-pourrissement*] of imperialism (of which the steadily deepening crisis is the first warning sign), the working class's struggle, if it is well conducted, will ultimately impose socialism and avoid 'barbarism'.

Even in that case, however – indeed, precisely in that case – Lenin's short phrase (the 'culminating stage'), taken together with Engels's ('socialism or barbarism'), casts a singular light on imperialism on the one hand and the future on the other. On imperialism: it is already putrefaction and can rot in place indefinitely, and more and more, until it attains 'barbarism'. On the future: it will be either socialism or barbarism, depending on whether the working class and its allies take power or are indefinitely subjected to the domination of the bourgeois class – hence depending on the way the working class's struggle can be led to victory by following a correct mass line and adopting correct mass practices. This is a way of repeating, for our future and thus also for our present, the *Manifesto*'s twofold phrase: 'history is the history of class struggle'; 'the class struggle is the driving force of history'.

No one can doubt that this phrase is directly addressed to us, militants of the national and international workers' movement. If we are not already aware of it, we will 'put our heads to work'[91] in order to discover what we still have to do.

The fact that this phrase is also addressed to imperialism, however, is something that is either 'very well known' or not known at all. If it is 'very well known', the reason is perhaps that it is not (always) known. I mean that the class struggle which is the 'driving force of the history' of class societies in general is also the 'driving force' of the history of capitalism; it is also the driving force of the last, culminating stage of capitalism comprised by imperialism.

That is the only thing that this short book purports to show: that *the class struggle is the driving force of the history of capitalism and therefore also of its imperialist stage.* Something elementary. Those who will learn nothing from it (either because they know it, or because they think they know it, or because they despise it) may close this book in all (good) conscience. The others may read it.

The author begs the reader's great indulgence, because he has not read all the books on imperialism! There are so many and such learned ones, written by specialists in economics! He consoles himself with the thought that Lenin devoted only a little pamphlet to this big question and that Lenin was no more an economist than Marx was. A sort of courage comes over you when you can shelter behind examples as illustrious as these, the more so as it is simply a question of once again explaining what Marx and Lenin have already explained to us extremely well, while having the audacity, perhaps – that is, 'the weakness of ceding to the strength of consequences' (Rousseau)[92] – to extend their arguments on one or two points.

I know that some will hasten to take this audacity for recklessness in order to assure themselves of their guarantees. But 'nothing ventured, nothing gained' holds in the sciences as well as the class struggle. I would ask that they reread certain citations from Dante which Marx used as the epigraph to the *Contribution* in order to let certain nasty critics know in advance what he thought of them. 'This sketch of the course of my studies in the domain of political economy is intended merely to show that my views – no matter how they may be judged and how little they conform to the interested prejudices of the ruling classes – are the outcome of conscientious research carried on over many years. At the entrance to science, as at the entrance to hell, the demand must be made:

Qui si convien lasciare ogni sospetto
Ogni viltà convien che qui sia morta.[93]
(To enter this place, one must shed all suspicion
And, on all cowardice, inflict (have inflicted) death.)

(This is the place to shed all suspicion
And, on all cowardice, inflict death.)[94]

On a Few Bourgeois Errors and Illusions

When one is face-to-face with imperialism as we are today, and when one talks about imperialism, one must know the following idea, driving it into one's head ten, twenty, one hundred times over: the greatest illusion that can affect the way one imagines imperialism is and always has been the same illusion about capitalism in general that Marx never stopped denouncing.

One must also know that Marx denounced this illusion as a *typically bourgeois* illusion that the capitalists can no more shake off than the poor can shake off poverty, because of the nature of capitalism itself, which leaves no way out other than this bourgeois illusion.

Here is this illusion.

This illusion has it that *everything* that happens, hence everything that exists, is *natural*. Capitalism exists: it's natural, it's in the nature of things. Imperialism exists: it's natural, it's in the nature of things. Bourgeois ideology is not surprised by the existence of capitalism: it's natural. Why is it natural? Because it's 'in the nature of things'[95] that capital should produce profit and so on, that capital should be remunerated by profit just as the worker is remunerated by a wage and so on; that everyone should receive according to what he contributes to production, the capitalist as a function of his capital, the owner of land or buildings as a function of his property, the banks as a function of the credit that they extend and the worker as a function of his 'labour'. If we delve deeper, if we say, 'But it hasn't always been like that', if we drive the bourgeois ideology of the 'nature of things' into a corner by remarking that the nature of things has varied and therefore can vary, we will find ourselves confronted with the last, the ultimate answer: that's how it is because that's how it is. The accomplished fact.

Let us not be fooled: there is a certain Marxist way of *accommodating* this bourgeois illusion by dressing it up in Marxist terminology. To be sure, one will explain that the capitalist mode of production is a 'transitory' mode of production (Marx), that its 'historicity', hence its precariousness, are inscribed in its 'structure' (Marx), because this 'structure' is beset by mortal contradictions.[96] Apparently, then, one has given up the argument about the 'nature of things' by showing that things (here, the capitalist mode of production) emerge in history, have a history and therefore will have an end, yielding, after a long transition, to a completely different mode of production in which there will be no more classes (the communist mode of production). Apparently, history has taken the place of the 'nature of things' and, behind this great substitution, the reality of the capitalist production process will appear: it is a production process that is at the same time a process of exploitation. Behind the 'natural' appearances of the 'it's normal that everyone should receive according to what he contributes: that the capitalist should receive a profit; the banker, interest; the owner of land or buildings, rent; and the worker, a wage', one will discover what Marx has shown us: the surplus value extorted in production by virtue of the working class's submission to exploitation and the 'division' of this surplus value into profit of enterprise (industrial or commercial), interest (bank credit and so on), ground rent (for farmland or other real-estate) and wages. Behind this facade of the 'nature of things', then, one will discover, as the basis for everything, the process of the exploitation of the working class by the capitalist class, hence the process of both the capitalists' class struggle and the workers' class struggle.

Here too, however, things can be turned around, very subtly, to be sure, but turned around all the same. We have to learn once and for all that the capitalist class is made in such a way (it is the capitalist mode of production that makes it the way it is) [that it] never lets go of its prey, will never let go of its prey, because it cannot let go of it without committing suicide, and because the capitalist mode of production is no more a suicidal mode of production for the class that benefits from its exploitation than is any other mode of production on earth. The capital class will never let go of its prey. This means, in the last instance, that it will never let go of the working class; by itself, it will never cease to exploit; by itself, it will never cease to wage the most consistent class struggle there is, from exploitation to the subtlest forms of political oppression, intimidation and ideological blackmail. Among other consequences, this means that bourgeois ideology will never let go of its prey, the working class itself, but will pursue it even in the class-struggle organizations that it has forged and is forging for itself, even in the scientific and philosophical theory of the struggle that the working class has conquered in order to carry out its own class struggle. The capitalist class will never voluntary cease to impose its domination even on the working class's theories and ideology in order to wrest from its hands and mind the very weapons it has forged for itself in order to carry its class struggle to a victorious conclusion.

The workers' movement has had long, hard experience of this operation of the capitalist class (carried out provisionally and over a long period, for it is constantly repeated, constantly begun anew), intended to disarm it by weakening its political line of struggle, its organizations, its theory and ideology; and it has acquired this experience at a terribly high price. It has given it names: reformism and revisionism.

We must not imagine that this enterprise of the capitalists' class struggle to subvert, divert and sidetrack the workers' class struggle is 'the most carefully meditated enterprise in the history of the human race' (Rousseau);[97] we must not imagine that it is conceived by the capitalist class's masterminds to carefully considered strategic and tactical ends. To be sure, the politicians who represent the bourgeois class and exercise state power on behalf of the bourgeois class as a whole are there for that purpose, and they do what they must, that is, what they can, consciously, deliberately. Yet they never do anything but serve a system (sometimes adroitly, but sometimes also maladroitly, for they do not know 'the law' of the system, given that they do not want to recognize it, cannot recognize it) that runs all by itself, inspiring their most 'conscious' thoughts.

For it is a one hundred percent bourgeois conception of the class struggle, the capitalists' class struggle no less than the workers' class struggle, to imagine this struggle as the struggle of conscious 'subjects' acting on a battlefield as smooth as a plain, as if they were generals on horseback equipped with spyglasses and taking such-and-such an action as a function of the enemy's movements. Once again, this kind of 'phenomenon' does exist, but it is the quintessential bourgeois illusion to believe that it is determinant in the last instance. The classes are not 'subjects'; although they act in their confrontation, they are 'acted' as much as, and even more than, they act – they are 'acted' by the laws of the class struggle, which is never reducible to the decisions of the struggling classes. Primacy of the class struggle over the classes, since it is the class struggle, its conditions and forms, that constitutes the classes as classes.

If this is indeed the way things are, when we say that the capitalist class never lets go of its prey, the working class, and never will, and when we say that it pursues its prey, the working class, as far as the political line of its class struggle organizations, as far as its theory and its ideology, this cannot be the simple effect of a 'decision' or 'resolution' – even lucid, even savage – of the capitalist class. For the capitalist class is not a subject. If this is the way things are, when we say that, under the impact of the capitalist class struggle, the working class is attacked even in its class organizations' political line and even in its theory and ideology, it is also not affected by this like a subject 'deviating' from its nature and line of conduct, a subject that would 'succumb to an influence' the way a free subject might succumb to an influence. Of course, reformism and revisionism can bear proper names (for, as a result of certain circumstances, such-and-such an individual becomes a historically decisive link and plays a key role in the process of deviation), but they can never be reduced to proper names.

The reason is simple: the working class does not, any more than the capitalist class, exist as a subject capable of taking wrong 'decisions' or of 'choosing' to follow an aberrant line.

The primacy of the class struggle over the classes holds for the working class too. How could it exist outside the couple capitalist class/working class? And if this couple constitutes the two antagonistic classes in their antagonism, how could the working class exist as a subject prior to the class struggle? In reality – this is what makes it very hard to analyse the 'deviations' observed in the workers' movement, and is no doubt responsible for the fact that the very word 'deviation' is equivocal, provisional and should be replaced – what occurs and is known as reformism and revisionism in the workers' movement, even if it is due to 'analytical errors' or, more profoundly, inappropriate (= incorrect [*non juste*], poorly adjusted) class positions, is, in the last instance, never anything but the effect of the class struggle inside the workers' movement.

Of course, to advance this proposition, we must have an idea of the class struggle altogether different from the generally accepted one. In particular, we must conceive of the class struggle as irreducible to the political and ideological class struggle and thus to the class struggle which can lay claim to the attributes of consciousness and decision in the dominant, that is, bourgeois, ideological depiction of it. We must conceive of the class struggle as a confrontation of two class struggles (*that* is the point: the class struggle is not the struggle of two classes each of which struggles against the other in their struggle because they are classes. Rather, it is the struggle between two struggles, the confrontation of two bodies both of which are in struggle, each struggling with its own weapons, which are absolutely not the same in the case we are examining, since the proletarian class struggle's weapons have absolutely nothing to do with the bourgeois class struggle's weapons and since the same holds for the strategy and tactics and practice of the struggle too), setting out from the domain of the infrastructure (from exploitation). We must also grasp that political and ideological struggles are not struggles of *ideas* (for 'idea' leads back to 'subject'), because ideology, to which politics is too often reduced, *is not ideas*, but practices in Apparatuses.

If this is so, we can now turn back to the bourgeois-ideological illusion that can endanger Marxism even in the way it imagines capitalism and imperialism.

For it is also possible to say of all that has been said that 'that's just the way it is'. To be sure, it will no longer be said that it's in the nature of things, since the nature of bourgeois things has now been replaced with the conflictual history of the class struggle. Subtly, however, the 'nature of things' can be surreptitiously transferred to history! One then lapses into an evolutionist conception of the Marxist representation of history. One marches all the modes of production down the grand Avenue of History, one after the other, the first pushing the second out ahead of itself, the second the third, and so on, down to the capitalist mode of production, which pushes its own (remote) future out ahead of itself: the communist mode of production. Thus history is strung together like pearls or engenders itself as in the beautiful genealogies of the grand myths in Hesiod or the Old Testament: so-and-so begat so-and-so, who begat so-and-so and so on *ad infinitum*.

We are now established in imperialism. Thanks to a quote from Lenin, which is also the title of his pamphlet, we know very well that imperialism is the 'highest stage' of capitalism. Supposing that we translate 'highest' [*suprême*] – where the elevation (there's nothing higher!) can blind us to the imminent end – correctly, as 'ultimate' or 'last', we will be aware that imperialism is the *last* stage of capitalism, the last phase in its history. In short, the last stop, after which it's 'all passengers are requested to leave the train'! For the capitalist voyage is over. And afterwards? We have socialism, which some, with their systematic imaginations, go so far as to consider a mode of production [*sic*].[98] In any case, however, if we believe not these scatterbrains, but Lenin, who never talks about a socialist mode of production, we have a very long transition under the dictatorship of the proletariat, which culminates in the communist mode of production.

Is this not in the 'nature of history'? Since history is the history of the begetting of modes of production by other modes of production in an evolution regulated by evolutionism, that is, by the necessary passage from the lower to the higher, from lower to higher forms, the lower engendering the higher within itself by the law of evolution which has it that 1. the course of evolution is never arrested; 2. there is neither void nor miscarriage in it; 3. every form naturally engenders the next; and 4. that, since each engendered form is higher than its predecessor, the course of things provides us with the guarantee that we're on our way to what's best. Under these conditions, Lenin's phrase is as reassuring and soothing as anything can be: imperialism is the last stage of capitalism, 'state monopoly capitalism is the antechamber of socialism';[99] we're at the end of the line. What is more, 'state monopoly capitalism' has gone into a 'global crisis'. Thus everything is unfolding according to plan, not the plan of the bourgeois nature of things, but the Marxist laws of 'historical development'.

There really is nothing more to do than wait. The trouble with this is the bitter experience of the people, which, when it is told about 'antechambers', cannot help making associations. For the people, an 'antechamber' (a notary's, a Minister's and so on) is a place where one can wait indefinitely. The expression *faire antichambre* [to cool one's heels] is the proof.

I affirm that, in this evolutionist representation of Marxist theory, we can hesitatingly recognize yet another victory, and a big one, of bourgeois ideology, of the bourgeois class struggle over the workers' class struggle.

But that is not all. We had risen above the 'nature of things' to attain the 'laws of history'. When these laws are impenetrable, however, because we have failed to penetrate them, do we not simply fall back to the level of the 'nature of things'?

What I mean is very simple. When someone draws up a 'chart' of imperialism's effects for us, tallies up its effects for

us, when he says that there is x, y and also z, without giving
us explanations (as sometimes happens) or while giving us
merely plausible, but not enlightening explanations – in
short, when someone plants imperialism before our eyes in
one big package, even if it's a neat package, even if it comes
with a few explanations or even a very subtle theory, but
unconvincing explanations and an unconvincing theory,
and if, on top of everything else, the theory is manifestly
wrong, do we not relapse into the 'nature of things'?

An example: imperialist wars. People cite the United
States' war with Spain and the first World War, together
with a few other undertakings of imperialist colonialism's
(the US War against Vietnam). The fact is that these wars
took place. This is sufficiently well known: people (not
everyone!) suffered enough as a result and generations
were marked in their flesh by these wars. But 'that's just
the way it is'. Fine. We know that these wars are imperialist wars, that they are among the effects of imperialism
and prolong monopoly capitalism's struggle to divide
up the world by force of arms. We know that they were
horrible, caused unprecedented destruction and massacred
tens of millions of human beings. To blame for them were,
assuredly, the Nazis, who were frightful sorts: 'the most
reactionary of all the representatives of finance capital'.
We know well where we are: under imperialism, which
means that the wars are imperialist wars for a new division
of the world. But a war is a war: it entails destruction and
death. That's just the way it is. It's in the nature of things:
we're on the threshold of that again, and on the threshold
of psychology to boot: the Fascists were frightful sorts,
'the most reactionary ...'. The word 'reactionary' gives
things a political ring, but it's a fake window added on
for the sake of symmetry: Why were the other (American,
English or French) imperialists *less* reactionary? And what
does 'reactionary' mean, if it does not simply designate
empirical practices that are in fact left unexplained?

For example: Why did the Nazis and the Fascists wage
what they called 'total war'? Apparently because they
felt like it. That's easy to understand when we start out
from their nature as 'the most reactionary', no doubt.

Why, however, did the United States do the same thing in Germany and Japan? No doubt because, being 'less reactionary', it was forced to by the Nazis' methods. Can a 'less reactionary' sort, then, comport himself in this fashion without becoming 'most reactionary', like the 'most reactionary' sorts? Strange. Suppose we appended a very small question to these remarks: Why is it that Marxist analyses of the Second World War maintain silence about the fact that this Second World War was, in its turn, an inter-imperialist war? Why is it that this second imperialist World War is most often described as an 'anti-fascist war', something that is true only of its subordinate aspect?

I affirm that when we fall back in this fashion, for lack of appropriate, that is to say, correct explanations, to the level of the 'nature of things', it is an unmistakable sign that the bourgeois class struggle has scored another point against the workers' class struggle, down to the very image of imperialism that the explanations furnished by the workers' class struggle organizations produce.

I could multiply examples. Let us take just one, that of the monopolies. Having read Lenin, everyone knows that imperialism and monopoly capitalism are one and the same thing. For imperialism to exist, monopolies must exist. Fine. Unless, however, we regard these monopolies as an accomplished fact ('that's just the way it is'), hence as the accomplished fact of the 'nature of things', we have to find a reason for their existence. It will be said that they are produced by concentration. Fine. This explanation, however, may be just words, for it merely shows that, before the monopolies, there existed smaller firms that became bigger by concentration, the bigger ones absorbing the smaller ones; this made the big ones that much bigger, to the point that they became monopolies.

That is not an explanation. It is merely a description which says 'that is the way it is'. The nature of things again. If you raise this objection and ask what the reason for this concentration is, this absorption of the little ones by the big ones, which become even bigger as a result, the answer will be 'competition'. The law of competition. Firms struggled with each other; some were unable to weather the storm and were absorbed by the others, who prevailed in the struggle. One then proceeds to unveil a whole social Darwinist world of the 'struggle for survival' which, not to trace things as far as Darwin, is singularly reminiscent of Spinoza's rule of natural law: everyone knows that, in the ocean, big fish eat medium-sized fish and medium-sized fish eat little fish.[100] Fish eat each other. That's how they compete. The difference from the capitalists is that the big ones don't get bigger because they've eaten the medium-sized ones, nor do the medium-sized ones get bigger because they've eaten the little ones. Competition among fish is a nutritional competition that doesn't lead to concentration, whereas competition among capitalists is competition among businessmen who acquire the volume of big ones when they devour little ones.

The trouble with this explanation – Marx comes back to this in *Capital* so often that it's almost indecent to recall it – is that it is a bourgeois explanation; the trouble with it is that competition is 'an illusion'.[101] Not that competition doesn't exist: it exists, however, at its level, as an effect, and as an effect governed by a cause that has nothing to do with competition. It doesn't exist as the cause of the phenomena in question; it isn't the essential cause, the cause in the last instance of the concentration of firms and their transformation into monopolies. To be sure, it plays a role in concentration, but this role is subordinated to, and governed by, the cause that commands concentration and also commands the competitive forms that contribute, at their subordinate level, to realizing it.

Was I wrong to speak, a moment ago, of bourgeois ideology's deformation, sustained by the 'illusion of competition', of the way the working class may sometimes imagine imperialism? Marx himself says this, in terms that are not open to challenge, because Marx, while he rejects 'the illusion of competition' as the ultimate cause of concentration, obviously does not leave matters at that. He tells us the real cause of concentration, in terms that also enable us to understand why 'the illusion of competition' is necessary and why this 'illusion' is necessarily bourgeois, that is, forms an integral part of bourgeois ideology.

He thereby makes it possible for us to understand that the infiltration or contamination of the explanation of monopolistic concentration by competition is another way in which the bourgeois class struggle makes inroads on the working class's representation of the reality of imperialism. Even under cover of history, which has apparently replaced the 'nature of things', it is, once again, the 'nature of things' that is put back in the saddle, not just in the form of the opacity of history, but in the form of its bourgeois explanation, which is clear as day; for what on earth is clearer than competition, the play of supply and demand, the struggle among capitalists and the struggle among different capitals for investments – in short, the struggle for survival?

Thus whether one invokes 'the nature of things' or 'the nature of history' either in its evolutionist form or as shaped by the self-evident truths as big as a barn door that it vehiculates (the big ones eat the little ones and that's why they become still bigger), one remains and will continue to remain in the realm of the 'that's just the way it is'. One accordingly considers all the phenomena of imperialism (and of capitalism in general, in all its 'stages') as 'natural', as things that can be taken for granted, that is, as sanctioned by *self-evident truths*. We know, however, that self-evident truths are merely the commonplaces of the dominant ideology – in the present case, bourgeois ideology. Nothing is more normal than the fact that bourgeois ideology thus manages to carve out a niche for itself in the theory of the working class, since that is the essential aspect of its function (as a dominant ideology, its role is to dominate the dominated class's ideology). The fact that the organizations of the working class and their 'organic intellectuals' (Gramsci) consent to this is, however, something else again.

Marx, as early as the *Manifesto*, pronounced the last word on this whole business: 'history is the history of class struggle' (for class societies); 'the driving force of history is the class struggle'. *Capital*, the first volume of which appeared twenty years after the *Communist Manifesto*, is simply a commentary on these prophetic sentences, and a demonstration of them. Until you have reached the point at which economic phenomena can be thought under the 'law of history' known as the class struggle, you will remain stuck in a representation of things that is, willy-nilly – even when it takes the form of a theory of history decked out with as many quotations from Marx as possible – subjected to bourgeois ideology.

It is necessary to know that it is not just the 'nature of things' that is bourgeois, but that an evolutionist conception, an economistic conception of history and a mechanistic conception of the classes and their struggle (first the classes, then their struggle) *are also bourgeois.* The radical line of demarcation lies here: referring everything to the class struggle as the cause in the last instance: not to an idealist conception of the primacy of the class struggle over the classes, but, rather, to a materialist conception of this primacy, a materialist conception of the conditions and forms of the primacy of the class struggle.

I said in a recent essay that this line of demarcation distinguishes revolutionaries from reformists and communists from those who continue to think in bourgeois ideology, even when they are versed in Marx and think in his terminology.[102] It is clear that we must add that this reformism does not fall from the sky and is not the simple effect of a subjective conceptual 'error', but the (provisionally) victorious result of the bourgeois class struggle at the very heart of the representations reigning in the working class's organizations. And, precisely because it is a question of imperialism, it is Lenin who said it: imperialism is such that it produces reformism and revisionism in the workers' movement.[103] I am not inventing anything. I could even provide the requisite quotations.

On the History of the Capitalist Mode of Production

Theses:
1. *There is, in the first instance, no history but the history of social formations.*[104]

2. One should beware of the term 'social formation'. It is by no means an equivalent of the ideological term 'society'. The term 'society' is ideological in that it is the mirror term of another: 'individual'. But the couple 'individual–society' is an ideological couple about which we may say, without going back to the prehistory of class ideology, that it has been established for us in its currently dominant form by bourgeois ideology and bourgeois philosophy (especially the bourgeois philosophy of history, which 'exists' in multiple forms in the philosophy of the Classical period: for example, in the form of 'Treatises of the Passions'). In the couple individual–society, what is in play and at stake [*ce qui joue et ce qui est en jeu*] is the problem of *founding* social relations that are already in existence or are to come into existence, that is to say, bourgeois social relations: the problem of the transition from 'natural law' to the social state by means of the contract. Bourgeois philosophical ideology is haunted by this problem of foundation, that is, the 'natural' (= de jure) justification of bourgeois legal relations as constituting the essence of every 'society', that is, every association of human beings in history. It doesn't give a fig about the rest.

The term 'social formation', precisely, can be the object of scientific treatment in that it has nothing to do with the ideological couple individual(s)–society, hence with the notion (which is ideological in this couple) of 'society'.

The difference leaps to the eye when we ask about the *specific form* of a social formation. Let us take an example. For a certain time now, 'capitalist social formations' have been in existence. These capitalist social formations exist in and under a specific form: the *nation-form*. Is this self-evident? It is not as self-evident as all that. In any case, it is a self-evidence that has to be 'conquered'. For slave-based or serf-based social formations exist in forms completely different from the *nation-form*. And everyone knows with what insistence Marx[105] and Lenin[106] showed that the nation-form would not survive indefinitely (even if it lasted a long time), but had to disappear. For the form of existence of communist social formations (or of the communist social-formation?) will assuredly not be the nation-form.

Why do capitalist social formations 'exist' in the nation-form? Because, in the last instance – and everything else is subordinate to it, however contradictory it may be – the nation-form is imposed by the existence of the *market*, the geographical area for the existence and development of mercantile capitalist production: not just the market for manufactured products (commodities), but also the market for means of production as well as the market for labour-power. This is the obligatory starting point, and not just the starting point, but also the obligatory material basis, inscribed in geographical space, of every capitalist social formation. And what is happening now, with the development of imperialism, which is going beyond the global market for commodities, because the global market for commodities is dominated by the global market for financial capital, and which is going beyond nations, because we are witnessing the constitution of 'multi-national' monopolies (one might just as well call them 'inter-national' monopolies); everything that is happening, as well, in the attempt to constitute a 'European market' common to several imperialist nations, at the price of what enormous difficulties – all this by no means abolishes the basic nation-form, but, on the contrary, presupposes it. It is on the basis of the nation-form, hence of the national market, that the 'global', 'international' and 'continental' (Europe) forms of contemporary imperialism are being constituted.

3. Thus it is in this sense that we can say: there is, in the first instance, no history but the history of social formations, in the awareness that *the form of existence of social formations is determined by the mode of production that is realized in them*. For each mode of production, there is a form of existence and realization of the corresponding social formation.

This distinction is crucial. For we can say the following: not every mode of production 'finds', automatically, by virtue of some sort of divine right or ontological argument (which would have it that every essence is fully entitled to exist, that every mode of production exists by virtue of its essence), *the form* in which it can exist. If it 'finds' that form, that is, if existing conditions allow it to endow itself with existence, to realize its existence, to 'forge' it, then the mode of production in question will exist. If it fails to find that form, if existing conditions do not allow it to realize it, to impose it, then the mode of production will not exist. Or if it has begun to exist for a time but, at the end of the prescribed period (for in these matters Spinozist necessity is unrelenting), has not managed to endow itself with *the form* of social formation corresponding to it, that is, the form that allows it to reproduce itself in either simple or extended form, then the mode of production in question will perish.

This has happened in history, doubtless a considerable number of times. The trouble with history (I mean the history of the historians) is that it 'works on' the accomplished fact and in the fetishism of the accomplished fact, hence on the durable result that is capable of producing the conditions of its reproduction, just as the biologist works on the species which exist, that is, which have succeeded in reproducing themselves. However, the biologist, at least, knows what fantastic waste life had to pay in order to succeed in producing (if I may be allowed this terminology of 'success') a few species capable of self-reproduction, such as man. What lives is what has survived: it exists only on a fantastic, unimaginable field of cadavers that were unable to live. Traces of them subsist in sedimented layers and fossils. That is why biologists have a vague notion of the history of life, and suspect that the mystery of life [*vie*], that is, of survival [*survie*], is to be sought not in what lives, that is, survives, but in what is dead, that is, has not survived. Historians, generally speaking, have not got that far yet.

Yet it is necessary to get that far in order to put an end, as is beginning to happen in biology, to the ideological theory of evolutionism in history itself. It is necessary to get far enough to consider modes of production that have died, have proven unable to survive because [they] were not able to reproduce themselves, since, among other reasons, they did not succeed in realizing the proper *form* of social formation in which the mode of production in question could exist. Not that there is an essence of the mode of production searching for the form of its existence: for the essence does not exist outside of this search for its proper form of existence.

To take just one example: Have we been sufficiently surprised by the fate of the fourteenth-century Italian cities that promised us the advent of capitalism, but whose 'destiny' miscarried? We must go further: they had well and truly 'realized' capitalism in both town and country, including quite modern forms of capitalism: assembly-line work running on hydraulic power in big industry, a task-based labour process and, in the countryside, utilization of existing scientific procedures to develop production (a whole corps of agronomists in the service of agrarian capitalists). Yet this capitalism died.

Why? Because the existing social formation, a city plus the surrounding countryside, was not the proper form for the development of the capitalist mode of production. What was required was the nation-form, when all that was available was the city-form plus a little countryside. Nothing with which to constitute the broad market that capitalism needed (the market in all the senses indicated above). This explains the death of these capitalist social formations. They died because they were unable to constitute the proper form for the existence of the capitalist mode of production, that is, for its simple reproduction and its reproduction on an extended scale: the nation-form.

If there was someone who understood this, and in Italy itself, it was a certain person named Machiavelli. I do not say that he said everything. He had understood, however, what the *missing* 'decisive link' was that had to be forged[107] – forged starting from scratch, if need be, starting from nothing: the nation. Hence *The Prince*. Yet the historians have not understood this. Have the Marxists themselves understood it? They strike the existence of capitalism in fourteenth-century Italian cities from history, because this existence followed by death disturbs them, because they vacillate between empiricism and the ontological argument and resolve their hesitation in evolutionism: what existed in these cities could not have been capitalism, because it died! And because capitalism, by definition, has to exist as the mode of production that follows the feudal mode of production. It cannot, therefore, have to exist and, at the same time, die! That is the point we are at.

This simple remark obviously opens up dizzying prospects. It is a matter of common consent among Marxists that a mode of production *can* die. It would even seem that it is the essential thing that Marx opposed to the 'eternitarian' or 'eternalist' illusions of the apologists (economists or others) for the capitalist mode of production. But beware! A mode of production can die only if it *must* die! That is, when it has *'exhausted all its potentialities'* or *'developed all the productive forces that it was capable of containing'*.[108] In short, when it has 'seen its day', that is, fulfilled its 'historical mission' (in the case of the capitalist mode of production: to 'develop the forces of production in an unprecedented way'),[109] that is, done its *duty* as a mode of production. But that a mode of production and, what is more, the same mode of production, should afford itself the luxury of dying before accomplishing its historic duty, before seeing its day and so on, and, to put it this way so as to push the point to its limits, that it should die before (truly, durably) existing – that is out of the question.

I am well aware that those of a political turn of mind will object that this absurd question is of no interest, that one works only on what is, that only what really exists is worth struggling over and that one cannot struggle elsewhere than in what exists. But is this little question really of no political interest? It may be politically of the greatest interest that there can exist *forms* of social formations that impede (to put it politely) the existence of a mode of production. Moreover, we have discussed just *one* form, whereas chances are good that there exists *a whole slew of forms* apart from the nation-form of capitalist social formations. It can be reasonably interesting, for example, to ask oneself *in which forms* (not just the nation-form) a *socialist* social formation has to exist so that the communist mode of production, which exists in it (Lenin) in an antagonistic relation to the capitalist mode of production (Lenin), may have real chances of *existing*, that is, of prevailing over the subsisting elements of the capitalist mode of production, while also preparing the forms of existence of this communist mode of production. No?

I shall not discuss what haunts this simple question. Or, rather, let us discuss it. If we must come round to thinking that the secret of the historical existence of existing modes of production (in their specific forms) is to be sought not so much in the accomplished fact of the conditions of their existence as – at least in equal measure – in the annulled, because non-accomplished, fact of the conditions of non-existence of the same modes of production (for these conditions have sometimes been the death of them), we have to hold both ends of the chain to understand the conditions of existence of a mode of production which exists: that is, we have to compare the cases of existence with the cases of non-existence (in the sense indicated above) and *think the conditions of existence setting out from the conditions of non-existence.*

This is not without political consequences, with all due respect to specialists of the accomplished fact. For (to come back to the case before us, socialism) it can tell us something about the conditions of existence of an embryonic mode of production setting out from the conditions of its non-existence. This contradictory situation is very interesting, for – what a surprise! – it simply repeats Lenin's theory on the 'transition' from capitalism to communism. In socialism,[110] the conditions for the non-existence of communism have all been met and are there for all to see: they are the subsisting elements of the capitalist mode of production. Of course, they exist in 'different forms' (Lenin),[111] as do the classes and the class struggle; of course, they exist in 'different forms' – Marx would have [said] 'transformed forms'. Yet they are there, and are not imaginary at all, but very real and active. And it is clearly on condition that we 'resolve', in the right sense (in the right direction, thanks to a well-oriented political line), this contradiction between the conditions of existence and the conditions of non-existence of the communist mode of production that we will some day reach the communist mode of production. As for those who think that everything has already been decided in advance (as the destiny of the capitalist mode of production was decided in advance as soon as it came into existence, the proof being that, when it happened to perish because the conditions of its existence had not been fulfilled, one says it never existed – it is so easy to suppose, in this way, that all the dead never existed!), they need only reread Lenin, who said: we can fall back rather than advancing towards communism; we can 'cool our heels' [*faire antichambre*] in a socialism which, because it has stopped advancing, retreats.[112] It really seems to me that Lenin had understood the interest of this little question about the conditions of the non-existence (or death) of a mode of production fairly well. I mean the *political* interest (for, thank god, Lenin, at least, was not given to speculation).

Thus there is no history, in the first instance, but that of social formations, defined in this way: by the *forms* (of these social formations) which realize the contradictory couple of the conditions of existence *and* non-existence of a mode of production, since the question of the *existence* of a mode of production in a social formation is posed only as a function of this contradictory couple: conditions of its non-existence/conditions of its existence.

4. We said 'in the first instance', and rightly so. For we must go further. It is not possible to remain at the level of a dualism: on the one hand, the mode of production as an *essence*; on the other, the social formation as realizing the *conditions of its existence* (or not). In proper Marxism-Spinozism, essence and existence do not exist on two different floors: the essence exists only in its existence, in the conditions of its existence. This does not mean that there exists, by rights, a prior adequation which *guarantees* the essence the conditions of its existence. Bad luck! History amply demonstrates the opposite: the fact that contradiction is the lot of the relationship between the essence and its conditions of existence.

That said, not all contradictions, obstacles and frictions are pertinent: there is waste, an enormous amount of waste in history, of incidental costs in history. We may nevertheless say that the better part of this contradiction, far from being foreign to the essence, is an integral part of it and constitutes it. In short, we may say that the essence of a mode of production is contradiction and that the contradiction between the essence and its conditions of existence, far from being external to the essence of a mode of production, is that contradiction's main form of manifestation. This can be rather easily explained (when we know the 'contradiction' internal to a mode of production, at least in a class society where it stares you in the face, because it exists in the antagonistic character of its relation of production). But let us leave this point here.

Thus if a mode of production 'exists' in the forms of a social formation suitable to its reproduction, not outside in the ideal heaven of pure 'essences', we must be consistent and say that if there is no history but the history of social formations in the first instance, there is, in the last instance, no history but the history of modes of production. This means that a mode of production has a history.

This silly little sentence will provoke a smile. To break down open doors that way! Of course, when someone has opened a door for you, the door is open, and all you need do is walk in. But it had to be opened. And the person who walks through open doors is rarely the one who opened them. He prefers to pocket the gain while annulling the locksmith's work by saying that he did no work at all on the lock, that the door was already open and that the locksmith 'broke down an open door'. No matter.

Yet it is not without consequences to say that a mode of production has a history, on condition, to be sure, that each of these words, which are concepts, is taken seriously.

For we have to know what a mode of production is, and that is by no means obvious. We have to know it, not in a vague, approximate way, but in a precise, rigorous way, for that is how Marx worked the concept out – in order to make it a scientific concept. We are indebted to him for most of the work and also for the wherewithal with which to pursue his work. There can, however, be no hesitation as to the nature of the work. It rules out all approximation and calls for the rigour of science.

Then we need to know what history is. Same remark here too. History is not a vague word covering more or less everything we like, but a concept that is precise and rigorous because it is scientific.

Obviously, all this has to be explained. What we have just said about it, however, is, as a stand-in, sufficient warning that it is a serious matter to write this short sentence: 'a mode of production has a history'. For, short though it may be, this sentence is serious. Serious in the sense of a science.

We shall show this by way of a few consequences.

It will be agreed that a historical social formation (for example, capitalist France, existing in the 'nation-form') is the existence of a mode of production (here, the capitalist mode of production). With, on the one hand, all the waste and incidental costs one likes for now (we shall be discussing them later and it will appear what a strange kind of waste this is); with, as well, the contradiction we have pointed out between the mode of production and the social formation, that is, between the essence of the mode of production and its conditions of existence and non-existence, a contradiction which, we said, is constitutive of the existence of the essence of the mode of production (we shall see in what sense later). All this is agreed, then.

It should also be agreed that the essence of a mode of production is constituted by its constitutive relation of production, an antagonistic relation that divides and opposes two antagonistic classes in their class struggle with regard to the possession or non-possession of the means of production and labour-power (in class societies). This was demonstrated elsewhere.

If this is so, to say that a mode of production has a history is to say that what constitutes it, namely, its relation of production, has a history. I am here using the language of the singular (thereby following Marx in the unpublished chapter of *Capital*)[113] rather than the plural, which is used unthinkingly ('the relations of production').

This plural can be legitimate when we are talking about a social formation, in which there are several modes of production, the old ones dominated by the dominant one: since we find several modes of production in it, we find several relations of production in it. In a single mode of production, however, there is just one relation of production. (Of course, it is multiplied in other relations, but these are not relations of *production*.) Thus a mode of production's relation of production has a history.

We can gather some idea of this, approximately and empirically, by recalling all the formulas that Marx uses to discuss the 'development of the relations of production'. It is not just the productive forces which develop; relations of production do too. But development is perhaps the index (just the index, for we are not evolutionists) of a kind of history. Another index: if the relation of production divides the classes into classes that confront each other in the class struggle and if the class struggle 'is the driving force of history', the connection between the relation of production and history is a direct one, by way of the classes confronting each other in their struggle. I say that these are indices, just indices, not explanations. We shall come to this. For the moment, it was simply necessary to familiarize ourselves, even if at a distance, with the idea that the mode of production has a history.

To break down yet another open door, however, let us leave our argument here, change registers, and state this obvious truth: there is no history (thus no history of social formations) but that of their mode of production and by their mode of production.

This requires us to touch on the question of history, that word into which everyone crams his self-evident truths, but which Marx treated as a scientific concept. Everyone knows that history is what happens, even when nothing happens. That old fox Wittgenstein even extended the thing to the world! '*Die Welt ist alles, was der Fall ist.*'[114] 'The world is' 'everything that advenes', 'everything of which it is a question', 'everything that falls' (in the sense in which one says in the journalist's trade [in French], that a news dispatch 'falls').

This, however, is where the difficulty begins. Not everything that happens is historical; not all events are historical. What, then, makes the difference, that is, sorts things out? Neither you nor I, obviously, nor even great men. Ah, yes: the historians, it's their job. But on what criteria? When we examine them at all closely, we observe that historians' criteria and judgements, the historians who swim against the current excepted, never do anything but register the criteria and judgements of history itself. Paradox: it follows that it is history which sorts the historical events from the others, history which says what is historical and, therefore, what history is. But is the history which says what history is the same history as the history on which it passes judgement? Yes: the judgements of history are judgements that history passes on itself. Amen.

It is here that Marx slips in his little comment. The judgements that history passes on itself constitute history as history. Granted. These 'judgements', however, are not divine judgements: they are the *results* of class struggles that oppose antagonistic classes. The dominant class's victory over the exploited class is a 'judgement of history' that history passes on itself; the historians of the dominant class write this judgement down in their books, while covering the vanquished class (1848, 1871), as is only appropriate, with the stipulations and adjectives of its defeat, so as to render it all the more submissive for having dared to rebel. If need be, they even explain to it in detail why it could not *but* have suffered defeat, so that it does not begin again. Judgement of history. The defeated class, however, can retain a completely different memory of its defeat and the massacre inflicted on it; the event it was made to suffer can pass a completely different 'judgement' on history: 'No, the Commune is not dead.'[115] The proof is that it has not ceased to live, from the 1917 Revolution through Lenin dancing on the snow[116] to the Chinese Revolution and certain episodes of the Cultural Revolution.

Let us conclude. Depending on the events of the class struggle and the results of their confrontations, history does indeed pass 'judgements' on itself, which are these results, interpreted in contradictory ways by the classes in struggle; for the case of these results *is pending*, judged as they will be by the process of the class struggle that has produced them. 'We have lost a battle, we have not lost the war', said a bourgeois statesman;[117] but Lenin had gone before him to say of the Commune's defeat, however predictable and atrocious it was, that it had been necessary to wage the struggle, even if it was lost in advance, for the victories of the future.[118] Such is the language of the proletarians. As for the bourgeois, if they win a battle, they cannot imagine that they can lose the war. This is in line with their logic: one cannot, after all, ask them to believe in their extinction.

It may seem that the idea that history is the 'history of the class struggle' can now be taken for granted. This makes it possible to understand what, in the last instance, passes 'judgements' on history: the class struggle. That struggle does the sorting out; and, since it is itself history and its driving force, it is understandable that it does so without having to step outside history.

On Imperialism and the Workers' Movement

Old Cerreti, in his *À l'ombre des deux T* [In the shadow of the two T's], is not dumb at all when he explains Togliatti's grand invention: the mass proletarian party, different from the so-called 'party of cadres' that Thorez is supposed to have defended, in the so-called Leninist line.

If one believes that the organizational forms associated with the political line of the workers' movement have not changed, one is wearing blinkers. It is generally admitted that they changed in the past, before Lenin, who did away with 'aberrant' or 'insufficient' forms, those of the Social-Democracy, with its organizational forms without cells, without shop cells, without professional revolutionaries, hence without cadres, and so on. As far as the present is concerned, however, the belief is that things were established once and for all with Lenin, and one decides, on the basis of criteria that he laid down, that such-and-such is acceptable and such-and-such is not.

So it is with the 'Italian school' that Cerreti discusses, as well as the French Communists' opposition to Togliatti's 'Italian line'.[119]

Yet the French too came up with formidable inventions during the Popular Front period. They invented a 'line' of broad union: proletariat + poor peasants + the ruined or waged petty-bourgeoisie (the middle strata, as one said at the time) + certain elements of the democratic, anti-Fascist bourgeoisie.

The French, however, had left the conception of the party intact. Thorez had, to be sure, transformed the Party's atmosphere and practices (in opposition to Barbé's and Célor's 'group' and its sectarianism[120] and the period of 'class against class'),[121] but not the conception of the Party. It remained a party of the Bolshevik type.

Togliatti changed the conception of the Party as well as its line. Why?

The reason is relatively simple: Italian fascism. The victory of the Fascist party, which had succeeded in creating a real mass basis for itself after all but wiping out the workers' organizations and massacring their militants, called for an ad hoc 'reply'. Togliatti's position was that it was necessary to change the character of the Communist Party, making it into a mass party (no more 'cadres', even no more 'vanguard'), and to agitate wherever the masses were to be found, in the fascist trade unions in particular. This led to different forms of recruitment and different organizational forms, with a different line: winning over the Fascists, the low-level Fascist cadres and, simultaneously, the Catholics and so on. A displacement in the direction of a mass party with *hegemonic* objectives even before the dictatorship of the proletariat!

This explains the strange Italian conception of hegemony according to Gramsci. Hegemonic goals – electoral, cultural and in the trade unions – with politics resulting naturally, in some sort, from the synthesis of these objectives, none of which are such as to put the accent, as Lenin did, on introducing the party into the very heart of the class struggle: in the factories. This 'hegemonic' politics produced impressive results, as Cerreti proudly says (but they were Pyrrhic victories):[122] 1. the Italian Communist Party is the leading Western party (number of members – but an Italian party member is a special, 'hegemonic' kind of member ...); 2. electoral results – but they have their own 'buffer' ...;[123] 3. some big cities in the North are governed by Communists, regional governments are in the Communists' hands, trade unions as well and, above all, cooperatives and so on; and 4. privileged relations, albeit with ups and downs, with intellectuals and with – Catholics.

The paradox of this 'hegemonic' line and organization is that, using the above-mentioned means, it exercises 'hegemony' over the middle strata and cultural circles (the Church, the intellectuals), *on behalf*, obviously, of the proletariat and poor peasants. However, the peculiar feature of this hegemony exercised on behalf of the proletariat is that it all but neglects the proletariat itself, which no longer has a political organization in the workplace, where it is exploited – and also neglects the poor peasants, who, as Cerreti himself says, have been partly 'abandoned'.[124] In sum, the Party, in which there are a great many intellectuals, not all of whom have Togliatti's 'class', exercises proletarian hegemony over the middle strata and cultural circles by means of the arrangements we have seen; it exercises it, however, in the proletariat's name, on a proxy that the Party's intellectuals assign themselves, in the proletariat's absence, its political absence. The proletariat is organized in the trade unions; this explains the unions' compensatory tendency to adopt political objectives, with the blessing provided by the grand memory of Gramsci's factory councils in Turin.

It is, however, glaringly obvious that Togliatti's line is of the nature of a historical 'parry'. What Togliatti conceived of made sense only for an Italy that was occupied and dominated by fascism, by fascist hegemony. To fascist hegemony, Togliatti had to oppose the line of proletarian hegemony. He also had, however, to adapt to the conditions of fascist hegemony. He had to fight on the enemy's terrain. It is no accident that the question of the unions is at the centre of everything: the Fascists had conquered and transformed the unions. Togliatti's stroke of genius was to say: we have to struggle inside the fascist unions. He pursued the same inspiration everywhere. Togliatti's line, the line of proletarian hegemony (a concept which, in Lenin, means no more than that the proletariat should exercise political leadership over its allies),[125] was a *counter-line* (in the sense in which a destroyer that is designed to destroy torpedo boats is itself a torpedo boat [*un contre-torpilleur est un torpilleur*]), defined on the basis of the accomplished fact of fascist hegemony in Italy, and the forms and sites of fascist hegemony. From this there flows a conception of the Party designed to oppose it to the line of fascist hegemony and to bring about this proletarian hegemony, which is in reality hardly proletarian and not hegemonic in the sense that Togliatti gave the word, for he believed that there was a continuity between this hegemony of the proletariat over its allies on the one hand and the hegemony that *comes after* the seizure of state power, and that it was the same hegemony. Not true.

The upshot is that the organizational forms and, above [all], the line of a party such as the Italian Party have been determined by the political avatars of a class struggle dominated by the forms of fascist imperialism.

One could find no better 'differential illustration', with respect to the forms of imperialism and the local events precipitated by it, than the difference between the French Party and the Italian Party. These differences are merely the differential effects of the forms in which imperialism has been realized in two countries that are as similar, yet, at the same time, as different as France and Italy. Moreover, none of this can be understood except in relation to the consequences of the first imperialist war (1914–1918). France was victorious, and it oppressed and exploited Germany, whereas Italy, exhausted by its war, in which it had gained merely a formal victory, paid for the others: it was the weak point in the imperialist chain and fascism's first strong point. Not by accident.

Thus the question that obviously arises is to settle accounts with this past now, and see where we stand. It would be absurd to pursue a politics that was 'fixed' and seemingly 'fascinated' by the transitory conditions of struggle imposed by the forms in which imperialism, fascist or not, was realized before Imperialist War II, or during it or after it. Of course, it takes quite some time to constitute a political party and there can be no question of putting everything back on the drawing board at every imperialist 'turning point' here and there. It is precisely one of the truths of the 'polycentrism' too loudly proclaimed by Togliatti and his comrades to put the accent on the fact that, since the forms in which imperialism has been realized are *different* in the different imperialist nations[126] (the basis for them: a very great *inequality of development*, which can go in both senses, depending on whether the link in the chain is weak or not: it can be belated or, on the contrary, premature – while we're on the subject, what is the theoretical basis for inequality of development? Lenin does not say! – but the answer is nevertheless to be found in what Marx says of the contradictory, unequal process of realization of the law of the fall in the rate of profit),[127] the forms of organization, decision-making and so on should also be different, hence endowed with autonomy. 'Polycentrism' is one of the political effects imperialism has on the international working class, and one of its victories. This does not mean that we should oppose it; it is a necessary evil which has its good sides ('counting on your own strength' or, to a certain extent, a decline in the domination of the USSR),[128] but we should also be aware of what it costs us. No more International. That too is an effect of imperialism in its present-day development.

All that has to be re-examined. If it is not, and everyone just marches down the path opened up by his own past, with disdain for his neighbour and without knowing why he has struck down his path, we are in danger of making foolish mistakes.

'The Pure Essence'

We are going to be discussing imperialism here not in this or that minor manifestation, but the way Marx discussed the capitalist mode of production in *Capital*, in its 'inner essence', *Kerngestalt* (central configuration), 'internal structure'[129] and so on; in short, in its 'ideal average'.[130]

The meaning of these terms that Marx never stops repeating in the course of his work has not always been understood. It has not always been understood why he was at such pains to warn his readers that he was only discussing this 'inner essence' or only discussing phenomena 'in their pure form', not in concrete detail. It has been the less well understood in that Marx plainly talks about real phenomena (such as profit, rent, interest and wages in [*Capital*] *Volume Three*, where he says that we are finally going to 'turn back to concrete phenomena' in their concrete character, as they present themselves 'on the surface of things',[131] frequently invoking concrete examples into the bargain (for instance, the working day, the factory laws, English workers' conditions of exploitation, the cotton crisis of the 1860s and so on).

Yet Marx does nothing other than what any scientist does. He 'isolates' the mechanism that he has succeeded in identifying as essential; he isolates it from all details that might alter its course in an accidental, not an essential way; and he analyses the phenomenon in its 'pure form'. Just like the physicist who analyses the law of falling bodies, to take a simple example, he ignores everything that does not concern the phenomenon in its pure form (friction and so on). He thus creates the conditions for true scientific experimentation; the fact that it is purely conceptual experimentation changes nothing here. It is indeed an experiment in which the scientist Marx allows the elements to vary after isolating them as pertinent.

Marx and History (1975)

When we read Marx, we have a very strange impression, similar to the one we have in reading a few rare authors such as Machiavelli or Freud. The impression of finding ourselves confronted with texts (theoretical and abstract though they may be) whose status does not come under the usual categories: texts that are always *to one side* of the place they occupy, texts lacking an inner centre, texts which are rigorous, yet seem to be dismembered, texts that designate a space different from their own.

Capital, for example. A theoretical, systematic text, yet an unfinished [*inachevé*] one, in every sense of the word: not only because both *Volume Two* and *Volume Three* are just fragments by Marx that Engels and (*Volume Four*)[1] Kautsky put together, but because it supposes a culmination [*achèvement*] that is other than theoretical, an outside in which theory would be 'pursued by other means'.

Marx reveals the reason for this strangeness to us in two or three clear texts in which he expressly gives his theoretical position the form of a *topography*. For example, the Preface to the *Contribution* (1859) expounds the idea that every social formation is so constituted as to contain an economic infrastructure (*Basis* or *Struktur* in German) and a political and ideological superstructure (*Überbau* in German).[2] Thus the topography is presented by means of the metaphor of a building in which the storeys of the superstructure rest on an economic basis.

We do not know many theories that take the form of a topography besides Marx and Freud.

What does this *topography* mean in Marx?

1. It points to a *distinction* in every 'social formation' (society) between the (economic) base and the (political and ideological) superstructure. Thus it brings out distinct levels of reality and distinct realities: the economic, the legal-political and the ideological.

2. This distinction, however, is much more than a simple distinction between realities: it points to *degrees of efficacity* within a unity. It designates the base as the 'determination in the last instance' of the social formation and, within this overall determination, it designates the 'reciprocal determination' [*détermination en retour*] of the base by the superstructure. Philosophically, determination in the last instance by the base, by economic production, attests Marx's materialist position. This materialist determination, however, is not mechanistic. For the indication 'the *last* instance' presupposes the existence of *other* instances, which can also determine in their order, and therefore presupposes the existence of a *play of* determination and *in* determination: this play is the *dialectic*. Hence determination in the last instance does not exhaust all determination: on the contrary, it determines the play of the other determinations by prohibiting them from operating [*s'exercer*] in a void (the idealist omnipotence of politics, ideas and so on). This point is very important for an understanding of Marx's dialectical position. The dialectic is the play that the last instance opens up between itself and the other 'instances', but this dialectic is materialist: it is not played out up in the air, it is played out in the play opened up by the last instance, which is material. In the topography, therefore, Marx inscribes his materialist and dialectical position.

3. But that is not all. In its form, the topography is something other than a *description* of distinct realities, something other than a *prescription* of the forms of determination: it is also a register of *inscription* [*tableau d'inscription*] and thus a positioning mirror for the one who states it and the one who sees it.[3] By presenting his

theory as a topography, by affirming that every 'society' is so constituted as to contain a base as well as a legal-political and an ideological superstructure and by affirming that the base is determinant in the last instance, *Marx inscribes himself* (his theory) somewhere in the topography, and simultaneously inscribes every future reader in it. This is the ultimate effect of the Marxist topography: it resides in the play or even the contradiction between the efficacity of a given level on the one hand and the virtual position of an interlocutor in the topography. Concretely, this means that the play of the topography becomes, by virtue of this contradiction, an interpellation, a call to practice. The theory's internal dispositive, insofar as it is *unbalanced*, induces a disposition to practice that continues the theory by other means. This is what lends Marxist theory its strangeness and what is responsible for the fact that it is necessarily unfinished (not like an ordinary science, which is unfinished only in its theoretical order, but in a different way). In other words, Marxist theory is haunted, in its theoretical dispositive itself, by a certain relationship to practice, which is at once an existing practice and a practice to be transformed: politics.

It seems that we can say the same thing about psychoanalytical theory, albeit in different terms. It too seems to be haunted in its theory by a certain relationship to practice (the cure). The fact that Freud had to think his theory in the form of a topography may well correspond to this obscure necessity.

That said, let us try to go a little further. What is Marx's contribution? What did he discover? He himself says, in the Preface to *Capital*, that he proposes to make an *analysis* (another term that suggests a comparison with Freud: Marx glories in the fact that he introduced the 'analytical method into political economy'),[4] an analysis of the capitalist mode of production. In fact, his whole *œuvre* is centred on this object, to which he is the first to have given its name of mode of production. In *Capital*, however, Marx also makes excursions into pre-capitalist modes of production, and he also discusses (albeit very briefly, not wanting to 'writ[e] recipes ... for the cook-shops of the future') the future communist mode of production.[5] In the Preface to the *Contribution*, he even sketches a kind of periodization of history in which the primitive communist, slave-based, feudal and capitalist[6] modes of production succeed each other.[7] Thus while Marx strictly limits himself to analysing the capitalist mode of production, he nevertheless considers past history as well and does not hesitate to write about history in the making, French history (*The Eighteenth Brumaire* and so on), the history of England, Ireland, the USA, India and so on.

Marx thus has a certain idea of history, not just a theory of the capitalist mode of production. He had already announced this idea in a famous sentence in the *Manifesto*: all history down to our day is the history of class struggle. To invest this sentence with substance and meaning, it would seem to be enough to combine [*rapprocher*] it with the succession of modes of production.[8]

Yet things are not so simple. For this combination [*rapprochement*] can give rise to several different interpretations.

One may say, for example, that the class struggle is the driving force of history and that, thanks to the class struggle – that negativity – history progresses from one mode of production to the next until it reaches its end, the abolition of classes and the class struggle; for each mode of production contains *in itself*, potentially, the following mode of production. In that case, one develops a Hegelian conception of dialectical development or an evolutionist conception of necessary stages: in short, one comes up with a philosophy of history in which history is an entity, a Subject, endowed with a Goal, a Telos, that it pursues from its origins, by way of exploitation and class struggle. In a conception of this kind, history always has a *sens* (in the two senses of the [French] word: a goal and a meaning). This conception is not Marx's. If there are ruses *in* history (ruses and mockeries), there is no ruse *of* history; if there are goals/meanings *in* history, there is no goal/meaning *of* history. This distinction between the *in* and the *of* is sometimes very hard to maintain; it is sometimes very hard to keep from confusing a *tendency* currently dominant *in* history with the goal/meaning *of* history. The integrity of Marx's materialism, however, comes at the price of this distinction.

For Marx was able to write *Capital* only on condition of breaking with every philosophy of history, and also with every (philosophical) theory claiming to account *exhaustively* for the *totality* of observable phenomena in human history. To understand this, we have to form an idea of what his position is and how he regards it.

We have to imagine Marx ensconced, I would say hidden away (the 'old mole' that is his foible),[9] squarely in the middle of the capitalist nineteenth century, and aware of it, and having attained an awareness of what capitalism means. This particular Marx, confined to the horizon of what he can know (and nothing more), straightforwardly writes: '*What is called historical development rests, in general, on the fact that the latest form regards the earlier ones as stages leading towards itself.*'[10] The representation of history is therefore 'spontaneously' haunted by an extraordinary illusion: that past forms were destined to produce the present. Since the present is the *result* of a *past*,[11] the present imagines that it was the *goal of* the past! And Marx adds: '[and as this] latest form' was 'only rarely, and under quite definite conditions', 'capable of self-criticism', it 'conceives them in a one-sided manner'. To succeed in escaping from the teleological illusion and its effects, the 'latest form' must be capable of producing 'its self-criticism', that is, of seeing itself clearly. 'The self-criticism of bourgeois society', as Marx puts it, may then make it possible to understand 'the feudal, ancient and oriental societies'.[12] This 'self-criticism of bourgeois society' is *Capital*, which was to a large extent written in 1857–1859. Armed with this knowledge, Marx could leave his hole and broach the strange thing known as history.

Marx's critique of the teleological illusion leads him to refuse to project *as such*, onto past societies, the categories that explain present-day society.[13] Depending on the case, some present-day categories are partially or totally absent in a given past social formation and, when they are present, they are as a rule *displaced* and play a different role. Even when it is similar, it is only such *cum grano salis*.[14]

This history, however, presupposes the *existence* of a certain past, which can in its turn be considered the goal of its own prehistory. The teleological illusion of history has to be pursued to its last refuge. Marx's little sentence is well known: 'The anatomy of man is a key to the anatomy of the ape.'[15] It means: assuming it has been factually established that man is descended of the ape, that man results from the ape, it is not (contrary to every evolutionism) the anatomy of the ape that will give us the anatomy of man, but the anatomy of man that will give us 'a key', and only one key, to the anatomy of the ape. To refer to a famous phrase of Hegel's, who insisted that one should never present 'the result without its becoming',[16] but who held that the becoming of the result already contained the result in itself, Marx would say: every result is plainly the result of a becoming, but its becoming does not contain that result *in itself*. In other words, if the result is clearly the necessary result of a becoming, the becoming that produced this result does not take the form of a *telos*. That is why 'the latest form' cannot consider 'the earlier ones as stages leading towards its degree of development'.[17]

This last idea leads us[18] to what I would call a counter-history, a negative history, as the ground and incidental costs of 'positive' history. History as it is commonly conceived is the history of *results* as stages in the becoming of the currently existing form, the history of the *results retained* by history: it is not the history of the non-results, of becomings without results and results without becoming, of abortive forms, repressed forms, dead forms – in short, of failures, not the failures that history retains, but the failures it does not. Official history, written in our Western tradition by and for the dominant class, is the history of a domination which crushes the other history, that of the shades and the dead. Yet history always advances 'by its bad side', Marx wrote in *The Poverty of Philosophy*.[19] With that, he breathed life into an entire repressed history; he revealed a becoming that had been without result until then, that of the exploited and oppressed masses, always good for all the drudgery and all the massacres:[20] the bad side. But, with that, Marx opened *the vast field of non-history* in all its forms, that of societies that have disappeared forever (results without becoming), that of miscarriages (capitalism in the fourteenth-century Northern Italian cities in the Po valley), that of 'antediluvian' existences, that of 'survivals', that of premature revolutions and many more histories in which oppression, repression, and forgetting vie with failure.

It is by combining the history of results and this repressed counter-history that Marx succeeds in thinking history differently, without resort to the categories of teleology and contingency.[21]

I shall, from a certain angle, try to answer the following question: Under what conditions is there human history? Or again: How is history rooted in a human group, in a social formation?[22]

For Marx, who does not raise the question of prehistoric anthropology, man is a social animal distinguished by the fact that he *produces* his conditions of material existence. Kant had already said that man is an animal who works,[23] and Franklin before him had said that man is a tool-making animal.[24] Marx cites Franklin in *Capital*:[25] man makes tools in order to produce his means of subsistence, in order to wrest them from nature by his labour. He does not, however, labour in solitude. There is a division of labour even in the most primitive groups, hence forms of cooperation and forms of organization of labour. Thus a human group or social formation produces its subsistence. If such-and-such a group *exists*, it is because it has succeeded in *reproducing itself* down to the present. That is the point on which everything turns. For this group has reproduced itself not just biologically, but also *socially*, by reproducing the conditions of production of its means of subsistence. In other words, *behind production*, which is visible and leads Franklin to say that man is a tool-making animal, behind the dialectic of labour exalted by Hegel, Marx points (after the Physiocrats) to a silent process which commands the first and is invisible: *the reproduction of the conditions of production.*

From a practical standpoint, this means, first, that production has to include a material excess, a surplus product, and not just any surplus, but a defined surplus that makes it possible to reproduce the elements of the process of production after each of its cycles: extra tools to replace those that have worn out, extra wheat for use as seed and so on. In short, an excess that is a determinate reserve for ensuring the reproduction of the material conditions of production (everyone knows that, for centuries, war was one means of ensuring this reproduction: war for land, slaves and so on). If these conditions are not secured by reproduction, the social formation declines and perishes. Where there is no continuity in existence, there is no history. If, in biology, to exist is, for a species, to reproduce itself, to exist in history is to reproduce the material and social conditions of production.

For the *social* conditions must also be reproduced, not just the *material* conditions (tools, seed, labour-power). The social division and the forms of cooperation must be reproduced and this presupposes an entire political and ideological superstructure capable of ensuring the reproduction of functions and their coordination in production. This can be seen in primitive societies in which myths and a society's priests play the role of regulating the social conditions of reproduction by sanctioning the division of labour, kinship relations, the rhythms and therefore the organization of tasks and so on.

Marx decrypted all of this, which has become familiar to us, in his analysis of the capitalist mode of production; it can, of course, be applied to pre-capitalist formations only *cum grano salis*. This unity of production and reproduction, however, and the superstructure-effect as a condition of social reproduction, are essential to Marx's idea of history, as is the distinction that he makes, early in [Part 7] of *Capital Volume One*, between simple reproduction (on the same basis) and reproduction on an increasing scale (on an expanded basis). There is no simple reproduction in the capitalist mode of production, which, however, reveals that it is possible. And it is no accident that Marx insists on the historical existence of *stagnant societies* that ensure their reproduction within the narrow limits of their previous production – that he insists on the historical 'ceiling' attained by pre-capitalist societies. Unlike them, capitalism is inexorably subject to expanded reproduction and to expansion across the globe.

Several conclusions can be drawn from this view of history:

1. We can understand the fact, pointed out above, that some 'societies' completely disappear: this happens when certain conditions for their reproduction are wanting for one reason or another. We can also understand that certain social formations aborted, such as the first forms of capitalism in Northern Italy (the absence of national unity = the absence of a sufficiently large market).

2. We can understand that in the 'societies' that have existed, history did not have the same pace, the same rhythm, the same 'times'; that there have been stagnant societies, others that have come to a standstill after a progression and still others destined to develop at a breathless pace.

3. Finally, we can understand the role of the superstructure, indicated in the Marxist topography. The function of the superstructure, the state and law, politics, ideology and all the works that are sustained by ideology is to contribute to the reproduction[26] of the social forms of production and, in class societies, to the reproduction of the social and ideological forms of the division into classes. We can understand at the same time, however, that the superstructure assumes and covers class violence only by sanctioning it by means of ideology, divine authority, the general interest, Reason or Truth. Material and social reproduction takes the form of the 'eternity' of ideological values, of which politicians are no longer anything but representatives. That is why, until Marx, history comes down to, and is reduced to, the superstructure; that is why there is an official history only of the superstructure, of great politicians, scientists, philosophers, artists and writers – in short, a 'one-sided' history, as Marx puts it,[27] a history which fails to penetrate the depths of the material and social conditions of production and reproduction, a

history that does not arrive at determination 'in the last instance'.

We can, however, draw another conclusion from this view, one bearing on the capitalist mode of production.

We have already noticed that history is not homogeneous for Marx, thanks to his remark that not just any social form has the capacity to produce its 'self-criticism', and thanks to his concern to avoid the spontaneous teleological illusion of history. Only societies in which the capitalist mode of production holds sway are capable of this. The reason is that the capitalist mode of production is not like the others, but unique in its order. It is distinguished by the organic feature, inscribed in its structure (valorization of value, production of surplus value), of reproducing itself on a *constantly* increasing basis, corresponding to its tendency to increase, deepen and extend the exploitation of waged labour-power without respite. I cannot go into the details here, but we can picture things schematically as follows.

In a certain way, all pre-capitalist modes of production have an 'open' or 'lacunary' structure, whereas the capitalist mode of production is marked by its *closed* structure. What ensures the closure of the capitalist mode of production is what Marx often calls the '*generalization*' of commodity relations, which is responsible not just for the fact that all products are produced *as* commodities, but also for the fact that *labour-power* itself becomes a commodity. In the pre-capitalist modes of production, commodities certainly existed, products which were sold as commodities, but they were not produced as commodities and labour-power was not a commodity. Hence an 'opening' continued to exist, a play whereby the lord exploited for his enjoyment, not to accumulate capital, while the serf could lead his own life, within certain limits and on the condition of certain forms of servitude. With the capitalist mode of production, labour-power becomes a commodity and the lord and master becomes a capitalist who exploits labour-power in order to accumulate capital. There is no possible escape from the relentless law of exploitation, the basis for the capitalist class struggle; no escape from the intensification of exploitation and the domination of the world. The destiny of the capitalist mode of production is a gigantic flight to the front; it is plunged into crises that are, for it, so many solutions obtained at the expense of the exploited, and it is subject to an antagonistic tendential law: it must keep increasing concentration and accumulation, while simultaneously educating the exploited masses and increasingly forcing them into class struggle, and also inciting colonized zones to seek their liberation; and it must live in this mortal contradiction until death ensues.

For Marx, this tendency is irresistible. Imperialism is the last form that it takes: the union of industrial and bank capital in the form of financial capital, the capital market's domination of the market for commodities on a global scale; a struggle between monopolies to divide up the world that culminates in imperialist war and so on. However, this irresistible tendency is not a fatality containing its solution in advance, without alternatives. Engels's phrase is well known: 'socialism or barbarism'.[28] The history that we have experienced invests this double exit with all its meaning. We can experience the irresistible tendency of imperialism in the forms of 'stagnation' (Lenin) and 'barbarism' (Engels), of which fascism gave us a preliminary idea. And this can last for a long time yet, for the characteristic feature of capitalism was already, and the characteristic feature of imperialism still is, an extraordinary capacity to transform its historic *crises* into historic *cures*: either to ensconce itself in the crisis, as in fascism or other, veiled forms of it, or to emerge from it, as in 1929, but by way of world war. The fact remains that in both world wars, 1914–1918 or 1939–1945, the imperialist world was only able to emerge from its crisis each time by paying the price of one or several socialist revolutions. For the alternative to barbarism can be socialism. For what is inscribed in imperialism's irresistible tendency is, *indissolubly*, at the same time as increasing exploitation and its extension on a global scale, the exacerbation of class struggle.

It is on this basis that it is possible to organize the workers' class struggle for the seizure of power and for socialism. Of course, there must be organizations of the workers' class struggle and they must know how to take up their place in the contradictions of imperialism at the Archimedean point: the one that makes it possible, not to move the world, but to change it.[29]

 5 May 1975

On History (1986)

Contrary to what Hegel, Engels and Stalin thought, but in conformity with what Marx thought (despite a few slips), there are no laws of history.

There is an individual and social historical necessity whose scientific theory can be elaborated: Marx's concepts of historical materialism and the materialism of the aleatory are proof of this. If there are no laws in history, there are lessons of history – but these lessons are themselves aleatory, for the same situation, the same conjuncture (Machiavelli, Spinoza, Marx, Lenin, Mao, Wittgenstein, Derrida), the same 'case' (Machiavelli, Spinoza, Stirner, Bakunin, Lenin, Mao and so on) is never reproduced.[1]

That is why Popper, the darling of Western epistemology, is right and wrong at the same time.

He is right when he recognizes that the human sciences do not proceed from [*ne relèvent pas de*] laws the way physics does.

He is right to say that every verification must be falsifiable, although he has a Kantian idealist tendency to formulate the conditions of the falsifiability of a statement a priori.

But he *is wrong* about the following points.

1. There can be no epistemology as a science of science (as a theory of theoretical practice) or science of the sciences.

2. There exists only a history of the sciences and the epistemological ideology which they produce, under the domination of which that history is produced.

3. That history, like any history, does not obey laws; we do, however, observe *invariants* in it (Lévi-Strauss) as well as their singular variations (Machiavelli, Spinoza, Freud). The theory of psychoanalytical or historical invariants, like the theory of topographical figures of the singular unconscious, like the theory of individual and social history,[2] can be, if it is taken seriously, a *falsifiable scientific theory*.

4. Thus Popper is wrong to deny history, psychoanalysis and the theory of the class struggle all scientific value; he does so because he is obsessed by the model of Galilean physics. Yet Heidegger denounced, and rightly, the exploitation of Galilean science by modern technology. Derrida has done even better, producing a theory of aleatory-materialist writing in his theory of the trace and the margins.[3]

To be sure, the human sciences (political economy, psychoanalysis, sociology) were, in their beginnings, 'theoretical formations of bourgeois ideology'.[4] However, since Comte and Durkheim, and above all Marx, Lenin and Mao, they have changed profoundly. Today, French and Soviet historians, Anglo-Saxon ethnologists and French philosophers are in the vanguard.

Read: [Rafaël] Pividal, [*Le Capitaine*] *Nemo et la science* [(Paris: Grasset, 1972)]; J[acques] Bouveresse, Minuit.

Soisy, 6 July 1986

Notes

Note on the Text

1 Part 1 of Althusser's biography appeared shortly after his death: Yann Moulier Boutang, *Louis Althusser, une biographie: La formation du mythe (1918–1956)* (Paris: Grasset, 1992). Part 2 should appear soon.

2 Louis Althusser, 'The Object of *Capital*' (1965), in Althusser, Étienne Balibar, Roger Establet, Pierre Macherey and Jacques Rancière, *Reading Capital: The Complete Edition*, ed. Balibar, trans. Ben Brewster and David Fernbach (London: Verso, 2016), pp. 237–67.

3 Louis Althusser, 'Letters to D.: Letter 2', in Althusser, *Writings on Psychoanalysis: Freud and Lacan*, eds. Olivier Corpet and François Matheron, trans. Jeffrey Mehlman (New York: Columbia University Press, 1996), pp. 54–77.

4 Louis Althusser, 'Portrait of the Materialist Philosopher', *Philosophy of the Encounter: Later Writings 1978–1987*, ed. Francois Matheron, trans. G.M. Goshgarian (London: Verso, 2006), pp. 290–1.

5 Louis Althusser, 'On Genesis', trans. Jason E. Smith, *Décalages*, 1/2 (2014), article 11, available at http://scholar. oxy.edu/decalages/vol1/iss2/11.

6 Pierre Vilar, 'Histoire marxiste, histoire en construction: Essai de dialogue avec Althusser', *Période: Revue en ligne de théorie marxiste*, September 2015, available at http://revueperiod.net/inedit-althusser-et-lhistoire-essai-de-dialogue-avec-pierre-vilar/; 'Marxist History, a History in the Making: Towards a Dialogue with Althusser', in

Althusser: A Critical Reader, ed. Gregory Elliott (Oxford: Blackwell, 1994), pp. 10–43.

7 Pierre Vilar, 'Histoire marxiste, histoire en construction', *Annales: Économie, Société, Civilisations*, 28/1 (1973), pp. 165–98.

8 Peter Schöttler, 'Paris-Barcelona-Paris: Ein Gespräch mit Pierre Vilar über Spanien, den Bürgerkrieg, und die Historiker-Schule der "Annales"', *Kommune*, 5/7 (1987), pp. 62–8. I thank Peter Schöttler for kindly putting the original French version of this interview at my disposal.

9 'Histoire marxiste, histoire en construction. Essai de dialogue avec Althusser. Tiré à part (dédicacé à Althusser) de l'article de Pierre Vilar publié dans *Annales: Économie, Société, Civilisations*, janv.–févr. 1973', Imec, Althusser Fonds, Alt2.A22.01–08.

10 There is a trace of this exchange in the editorial notes to 'Soutenance d'Amiens', in Louis Althusser, *Solitude de Machiavel et autres textes*, ed. Yves Sintomer (Paris: Presses universitaires de France, Actuel Marx confrontations, 1998), pp. 233–4.

11 Pierre Vilar, *Une histoire en construction: Approche marxiste et problématiques conjoncturelles* (Paris: Seuil/Gallimard, 1983). 'Marxist History, a History in the Making: Towards a Dialogue with Althusser' stands at the end of this volume.

12 Louis Althusser, *How to Be a Marxist in Philosophy*, ed. and trans. G.M. Goshgarian (London: Bloomsbury, 2017), p. 101.

13 Louis Althusser, *Filosofía y marxismo: Entrevista a Louis Althusser por Fernanda Navarro* (Mexico City: Siglo XXI, 1988).

14 Louis Althusser, 'Sobre el historicismo', in ibid., pp. 89–97.

15 Louis Althusser, 'Philosophie et marxisme', in Althusser, *Sur la philosophie* (Paris: Gallimard/NRF, L'infini, 1994), pp. 13–79; 'Philosophy and Marxism', in Althusser, *Philosophy of the Encounter*, pp. 251–89.

16 Louis Althusser, Letter of 15 August 1973 to Franca Madonia, *Lettres à Franca, 1961–1973*, eds. Yves Moulier-Boutang and François Matheron (Paris: Stock/Imec, 1998), p. 806. In a letter to Hélène Rytmann, Althusser boasts of how quickly he was able to resolve the theoretical problems posed by imperialism: Louis Althusser, undated letter to

Hélène Rytmann [28 August 1973], *Lettres à Hélène, 1947–1980*, ed. Olivier Corpet (Paris: Grasset, 2011), p. 636.

17 I have given this title to the chapter following a suggestion of François Matheron's.

18 In English, the two essays that first appeared in Louis Althusser, *Éléments d'auto-critique* (Paris: Hachette, Analyse, 1974), 'Elements of Self-Criticism' and 'On the Evolution of the Early Marx', were collected with two others in Louis Althusser, *Essays in Self-Criticism* (London: New Left Books, 1976).

19 Louis Althusser, undated letter [28 August 1973] to Hélène Rytmann, *Lettres à Hélène*, p. 639.

20 Ibid., pp. 639–40; Louis Althusser, Letter of 16 August 1973 to Étienne Balibar; Letter of 18 August 1973 to Étienne Balibar; Undated letter [autumn 1973?] to Pierre Macherey, in 'Correspondance au sujet de la collection "Analyse" dirigée par L.A.', Imec, Althusser Fonds, Alt2. A45–02.02. In 1980, Althusser and Hachette were planning to revive the series 'Analyse'.

21 Louis Althusser, Undated letter [28 August 1973] to Hélène Rytmann, *Lettres à Hélène*, pp. 639–40.

22 Pierre Macherey's suggestion to divide 'Analyse' into different sub-series (Louis Althusser, undated letter [autumn 1973?] to Macherey) helped Althusser to overcome his hesitation to launch 'Analyse' with a pair of books aimed at specialists of literature and linguistics: Renée Balibar with Geneviève Merlin and Gille Tret, *Les français fictifs* and Renée Balibar and Dominique Laporte, *Le français national*, both published in the sub-series 'Language and Literature'. See Althusser, Undated letter [28 August 1973] to Hélène Rytmann, *Lettres à Hélène*, p. 640.

23 Louis Althusser, *Les Vaches noires: Interview imaginaire (le malaise du Vingt-deuxième Congrès)* (Paris: Presses Universitaires de France, 2016), pp. 391–414. English translation forthcoming from Verso.

A Conversation on Literary History

1 Jean-Pierre Richard, *L'Univers imaginaire de Mallarmé* (Paris: Seuil, 1961) and Richard, *Stéphane Mallarmé et*

son fils Anatole (Paris: Seuil, 1961). These were Richard's principal and complementary doctoral dissertations.

2   There is a blank here in the transcription.

3   Henri Guillemin wrote several books about Rousseau, among them '*Cette affaire infernale*': *L'affaire Rousseau–David Hume, 1766* (Paris: Plon, 1942).

4   The transcription reads 'psychological'.

5   Charles Mauron, *Introduction to the Psychoanalysis of Mallarmé*, trans. Archibald Henderson, Jr. and Will L. McLendon (Berkeley, CA: University of California Press, 1963 [1950]); Mauron, *Des métaphores obsédantes au mythe personnel: Introduction à la psychocritique (Mallarmé–Baudelaire–Nerval–Valéry)* (Paris: José Corti, 1963).

6   Roland Barthes, *On Racine*, trans. Richard Howard (New York: Hill and Wang, 1964). On 7 May 1963, Barthes sent a copy of *Sur Racine* to Althusser, who had read it by the following day. Louis Althusser, Letter of 8 May 1963 to Franca Madonia, *Lettres à Franca*, pp. 412–13.

7   The transcription reads 'word' [*mot*].

8   Paul Éluard, 'Confections', no. 10, *Œuvres complètes*, vol. 1, eds. M. Dumas and L. Scheler (Paris: Gallimard, Bibliothèque de la Pléiade, 1968), p. 301.

9   There is a blank space here in the transcription.

10 The transcription reads: 'that is to say, historically a rejection' [*c'est-à-dire un refus historiquement*].

11 The transcription reads: 'they don't turn out anything' [*ils ne sortent rien*]. The mistranscribed phrase might also have been 'they don't emerge from nothing' [*ils ne sortent de rien*].

12 '"Béranger," said Goethe, "is a man most happily endowed. ... His affectionate admiration of Napoleon, and his reminiscences of the great warlike deeds performed under him ... these are things to which we cannot refuse hearty sympathy"'. Johann Wolfgang von Goethe, *Conversations with Eckermann (1823–1832)*, trans. John Oxenford (San Francisco, CA: North Point Press, 1984), p. 290.

13 'After judging him relatively mildly, Flaubert ended up truly execrating him' (my translation). É.L. Ferrère, *L'esthétique de Gustave Flaubert* (Paris: Conard, 1913), p. 113. 'I consider the aforementioned Béranger to be a bane. ...

But France is perhaps incapable of drinking stronger wine! Béranger [will be] its poet for a long time to come' (my translation). Gustave Flaubert, Letter of 9 August 1864 to Amélie Bosquet, *Œuvres complètes*, ed. Société des Études littéraires françaises (Paris: Club de l'Honnête homme, 1975), vol. 14, p. 211.

14 'Yes, 'tis a garret ... Come to mine eyes, ye dreams of love and fun ... In the brave days when I was twenty-one.' Pierre-Jean de Béranger, 'The Garret', trans. W.M. Thackeray, *Béranger's Poems in the Versions of the Best Translators*, ed. William S. Walsh (Philadelphia, PA: J.B. Lippincott, 1889), pp. 17–19.

15 See Louis Althusser, *For Marx*, trans. Ben Brewster (London: Verso, 1969), p. 126.

16 'If we were to build the cities today, we'd build them in the countryside; the air would be healthier there' (my translation). Jean-Louis Auguste Commerson, *Pensées d'un emballeur pour faire suite aux Maximes de François de La Rochefoucauld* (Paris: Martinon, 1851), p. 124. This witticism is often attributed to Alphonse Allais.

17 The transcription, corrected by hand here, reads 'evoked' [*évoqué*].

18 Michel de Montaigne, *The Complete Essays*, ed. and trans. M.A. Screech (London: Penguin, 2003), 125–31, 231–41, 521–2, 1226–9.

19 Alain Michel, 'La poétique du voyage: D'Homère à la modernité', in *Les voyages: Rêves et réalités. VIIèmes Entretiens de la Garenne Lemot*, ed. Jackie Pigeaud (Rennes: Presses universitaires de Rennes, 2016), p. 17: '[This] saying was making the rounds in the *hypokhâgne* in Marseilles when I entered it [shortly after the liberation of France]' (my translation). See Louis Althusser, *Philosophy for Non-Philosophers*, ed. and trans. G.M. Goshgarian (London: Bloomsbury, 2017 [1977]), p. 47.

20 Michel Foucault, *Madness and Civilization: A History of Insanity in the Age of Reason*, trans. Richard Howard (New York: Random House, Vintage, 1965).

Supplementary Note on History

1 Althusser, *For Marx*, pp. 117ff., 136–7; Althusser, 'The Object of *Capital*', pp. 237ff., 255ff.

On Genesis

1   The reference is very probably to 'Letters to D.: Letter 2', in Althusser, *Writings on Psychoanalysis*, pp. 54–77.

2   Karl Marx, 'Economic Manuscripts of 1857–58' (hereafter *Grundrisse*), *Marx and Engels Collected Works* (hereafter MECW) 28, pp. 421–2. See *Capital Volume Two*, MECW 36, pp. 38–9; Étienne Balibar, 'On the Basic Concepts of Historical Materialism', in Althusser et al., *Reading Capital*, p. 448, 451–2.

3   Jean-Paul Sartre, *Critique of Dialectical Reason, vol. 1: Theory of Practical Ensembles*, trans. Alan Sheridan-Smith (London: New Left Books, 1966), pp. 33ff.

How Can Something Substantial Change?

1   *Confédération générale du travail*, the largest French labour-union confederation, closely allied with the Communist Party in this period.

To Gretzky

1   Heraclitus, *The Cosmic Fragments*, ed. G.S. Kirk (Cambridge: Cambridge University Press, 1954), pp. 367–80.

2   See Louis Althusser, 'On the Objectivity of History (Letter to Paul Ricœur)', trans. Charles Gelman, *Décalages*, vol. 2/2 (2018), available at https://scholar.oxy.edu/decalages/vol2/iss2/2. In this reply to an essay of Ricœur's, 'Objectivity and Subjectivity in History', in *History and Truth*, trans. Charles Kelbley (Evanston, IL: Northwestern University Press, 2007), pp. 21–40, Althusser develops a critique of Raymond Aron, *Introduction to the Philosophy of History: An Essay on the Limits of Historical Objectivity*, trans. George W. Irwin (Westport, CT: Greenwood Press, 1976 [1938]). See also Aron, *Essai sur la théorie de l'histoire dans l'Allemagne contemporaine: La philosophie critique de l'histoire* (Paris: Vrin, 1938) and Aron, *Main Currents in Sociological Thought*, 2 vols, trans. Richard Howard and Helen Weaver (London: Transaction, 1998–1999).

3   Antonio Gramsci, *Selections from the Prison Notebooks*, ed. and trans. Quintin Hoare and Geoffrey Nowell-Smith (New York: International Publishers, 1971), Notebook 11, §27, p. 465. See also Antonio Gramsci, *Prison Notebooks*,

ed. Joseph Buttigieg, vol. 3 (New York: Columbia University Press, 2010), Notebook 8, §204, p. 352. Cf. Notebook 15, §61.

4 Vladimir Lenin, *Materialism and Empirio-criticism: Critical Comments on a Reactionary Philosophy*, in Lenin, *Collected Works* (hereafter LCW), (www.marx2mao.com: Digital Reprints, 2010), vol. 14, pp. 131–7. See Althusser, 'Is it Simple to Be a Marxist in Philosophy?', p. 193.

5 Karl Marx, Friedrich Engels[, Moses Hess, Joseph Weydemeyer], *The German Ideology*, MECW 5, pp. 39–40.

6 Plato, 'Theaetetus', trans. F.M. Cornford, in *The Collected Dialogues of Plato, Including the Letters*, eds. Edith Hamilton and Huntington Cairns, Princeton, NJ: Princeton University, Bollingen Series 71, 1969, pp. 887–8 (Theaetetus = pp. 845–919), 182a–183b.

7 Althusser is perhaps thinking of Raymond Aron, *Main Currents in Sociological Thought*, vol. 1, pp. 210–11.

8 Althusser, 'The Object of *Capital*', p. 253; Louis Althusser, 'The Historical Task of Marxist Philosophy', in Althusser, *The Humanist Controversy and Other Writings*, ed. François Matheron, trans. G.M. Goshgarian (London: Verso, 2003), pp. 210–11.

9 Blaise Pascal, *Pensées*, trans. W.F. Trotter (New York: E.P. Dutton, 1958), no. 294, p. 84.

10 See Althusser, 'The Object of *Capital*', p. 268; Louis Althusser, 'The Humanist Controversy', in Althusser, *The Humanist Controversy and Other Writings*, ed. François Matheron, trans. G.M. Goshgarian (London: Verso, 2003), pp. 232–3.

Draft of a Reply to Pierre Vilar

1 Pierre Vilar, 'Marxist History, a History in the Making', *New Left Review* 80 (1973), pp. 65–106.

2 Vladimir Lenin, 'On the Significance of Militant Materialism', LCW 33 (Moscow, Progress Publishers, 1973), pp. 232ff; Louis Althusser, 'Philosophy and the Spontaneous Philosophy of the Scientists', trans. Warren Montag, in Althusser, *Philosophy and the Spontaneous Philosophy of the Scientists and Other Essays*, ed. Gregory Elliott (London: Verso, 1990), pp. 131ff. First published in 1974, 'Philosophy and the Spontaneous Philosophy of the

Scientists' contains four of the five lectures that Althusser delivered in November–December 1967 in a 'philosophy course for scientists' that he taught with five colleagues at the Paris École normale supérieure. Mimeographs of these lectures circulated widely from 1967 on.

3   Karl Marx, *Capital Volume Three*, MECW 37, p. 804; Karl Marx, Letter of 27 June 1867 to Friedrich Engels, MECW 42, p. 390; Karl Marx, Letter of 11 July 1868 to Ludwig Kugelmann, MECW 43, p. 69.

4   Karl Marx, *Grundrisse*, Introduction, MECW 28, pp. 38ff, 43; Karl Marx, Letter of 2 April 1858 to Friedrich Engels, MECW 40, pp. 300–1.

5   The manuscript reads 'anti-humanism'.

Book on Imperialism

1   The famous phrase 'socialism or barbarism', which Rosa Luxemburg attributes to Engels in a pamphlet published in 1916, harks back, like a strikingly similar expression in an article of Lenin's published in 1915, to a formula of Karl Kautsky's. Luxemburg, 'The Junius Pamphlet: The Crisis in German Social Democracy', in *The Rosa Luxemburg Reader*, eds. Peter Hudis and Kevin B. Anderson (New York: Monthly Review Press, 2004), p. 321; Lenin, 'The State of Affairs in Russian Social-Democracy', LCW 21, 285; Kautsky, *Das Erfurter Programm* (Berlin: Dietz, 1965 [1892]), p. 141.

2   'To my readers' ends here, probably unfinished. Althusser develops the subjects he broaches in it in a chapter of *Book on Imperialism* that was probably intended as a new version of the opening of the book: 'Barbarism? Fascism was a Preliminary Form of It', p. 110 this volume.

3   Karl Kautsky, *The Agrarian Question in Two Volumes*, trans. Pete Burgess (London: Zwan, 1988).

4   Althusser left a blank in the manuscript here and filled it in later with the name Mehring.

5   Franz Mehring, *Karl Marx: The Story of His Life*, trans. Edward Fitzgerald (Atlantic Highlands, NJ: Humanities Press, 1981).

6   Vladimir Lenin, 'Notes of a Publicist: Catching Foxes: Levi and Serrati', LCW 33, p. 210.

7   The quoted phrase comes from another early work of

Lenin's, 'Our Programme', LCW 4, p. 211. Cf. Lenin, *What the 'Friends of the People' Are and How They Fight the Social-Democrats*, LCW 1, p. 146. In Althusser's French translation, the term corresponding to the MECW's 'foundation stone' is 'corner-stones'.

8   Althusser is perhaps thinking of Lenin, *Materialism and Empirio-criticism*, p. 20.

9   Nikolai Bukharin, *Historical Materialism: A System of Sociology* (Ann Arbor, MI: University of Michigan Press, 1969).

10   Raymond Aron, *Le Marxisme de Marx*, eds. Jean-Claude Casanova and Christian Bachelier (Paris: Éditions de Fallois, 2002 [1963]), pp. 346–8, 375, 447–62; Aron, *Main Currents in Sociological Thought*, vol. 1, pp. 164–9; Aron, *D'une Sainte famille à l'autre. Essais sur les marxismes imaginaires* (Paris: Gallimard/NRF, Les Essais, 1969), pp. 175–204, 298.

11   Lenin, *What the 'Friends of the People' Are*, pp. 165ff. See Althusser, 'On the Objectivity of History', p. 7.

12   '"There is no socialist mode of production" – thesis advanced by Althusser in a course on Marx's *Zur Kritik der politischen Ökonomie* … in June 1973.' Grahame Lock, 'Is it Simple to Be a Marxist in Philosophy', p. 17n. Cf. Maurice Décaillot, *Le Mode de production socialiste: Essai théorique* (Paris: Éditions sociales, 1973).

13   See p. 67 this volume. Cf. Vladimir Lenin, 'A Great Beginning: Heroism of the Workers in the Rear. "Communist Subbotniks"', LCW 29, p. 429; 'Better Fewer, but Better', LCW 33, p. 488.

14   Karl Marx, *Economic and Philosophic Manuscripts of 1844*, MECW 3, p. 313.

15   Ibid., pp. 294–5; Karl Marx and Friedrich Engels, *Manifesto of the Communist Party*, MECW 6, p. 487; Karl Marx, *Capital Volume One*, MECW 35, pp. 397ff, 491–2, 611n3.

16   Claude Meillassoux, *Anthropologie économique des Gouro de Côte d'Ivoire: De l'économie de subsistance à l'agriculture commerciale* (Paris: École des hautes études en sciences sociales/Mouton et Co., Le monde d'outre-mer passé et présent, 1964), pp. 168ff; Emmanuel Terray, *Marxism and Primitive Society: Two Studies*, trans. Mary Klopper (New York: Monthly Review Press, 1972), p. 96n; Pierre

Philippe Rey, *Colonialisme, néocolonialisme et transition au capitalisme: Exemple de la 'Comilog' au Congo-Brazzaville* (Paris: Maspero, Économie et socialisme, 1971), pp. 31ff.

17 Karl Marx, *Capital Volume One*, pp. 484–7; 'Critique of the Gotha Programme', MECW 24, p. 98.

18 Karl Marx, 'To Ludwig Feuerbach in Bruckberg', Letter of 11 August 1844, MECW 3, p. 355; Marx, *Economic and Philosophic Manuscripts of 1844*, p. 313; Karl Marx, *The Holy Family or Critique of Critical Criticism*, MECW 4, pp. 52–3; Karl Marx, *The Poverty of Philosophy: Answer to the 'Philosophy of Poverty' by M. Proudhon*, MECW 6, pp. 210–11; Karl Marx, 'Wages', MECW 6, pp. 435–6.

19 Marx and Engels, *The Communist Manifesto*, MECW 7, pp. 494–5; Marx, *Capital Volume One*, pp. 492–3.

20 See above, n. 14.

21 Karl Marx, *The Class Struggles in France*, MECW 10, p. 110; Marx, *Capital Volume Three*, pp. 434–5; Karl Marx, 'Marx to Nikolai Danielson in Saint Petersburg', Letter of 19 February 1881, MECW 46, p. 63; Marx, Letter to Friedrich Engels of 2 April 1858, p. 298.

22 Karl Marx, *The Civil War in France: Address of the General Council of the International Workingmen's Association*, MECW 22, p. 335; Marx, *Capital Volume Three*, p. 386; Marx, 'Inaugural Address of the Working Men's International Association', MECW 20, pp. 11–12.

23 Marx, *Capital Volume One*, pp. 317ff, 749–51; Marx, *Capital Volume Three*, p. 263; Karl Marx, 'Chapter Six: Results of the Direct Production Process', *Capital Book I, The Production Process of Capital*, MECW 34, pp. 428–9.

24 LIP, based in Besançon, France, is a company that manufactures watches and other time-pieces. On 12 June 1973, in order to prevent a Swiss multinational that had gained a majority on its board of directors from breaking up the company and laying off a third of the workforce, LIP's employees occupied their factory and, six days later, decided to take charge of production, under the slogan: 'we can do it: we can produce and sell ourselves'. Forcibly evacuated in mid-August, they regrouped in a gymnasium, where they continued to produce watches with a view to selling them illegally. The present chapter of *Book on Imperialism* is dated 17–18 August.

25 'Never before ... have the general secretaries of the two labour-union confederations in which three out of four workers put their trust ... spoken side-by-side on the site of a social conflict. That is what Georges Séguy [General secretary of the *Confédération général du travail* and member of the Communist Party's Political Bureau] and Edmond Maire [General secretary of the *Confédération française du travail*] will do this morning in Besançon [before the striking LIP workers].' 'La France à l'heure LIP', *L'Humanité*, 16 August 1973, p. 1.

26 The mistral is a strong wind that blows from the north toward the Mediterranean in Marseille and its environs.

27 Friedrich Engels, Preface, *Capital Volume Three*, p. 16.

28 See Althusser, 'The Object of *Capital*', p. 262; Louis Althusser, 'Chronologie et avertissement aux lecteurs du Livre 1 du *Capital*', in Karl Marx, *Le Capital, Livre I*, trans. Joseph Roy (Paris: Garnier–Flammarion, 1969), p. 19.

29 Cf. Louis Althusser, 'The Underground Current', in *Philosophy of the Encounter*, pp. 197–203.

30 See Louis Althusser, 'Appendix: On the Primacy of the Relations of Production over the Productive Forces', in Althusser, *On the Reproduction of Capitalism: Ideology and Ideological State Apparatuses*, ed. Jacques Bidet, trans. G.M. Goshgarian (London: Verso, 2014), pp. 209–17.

31 Marx, *Grundrisse*, Introduction, MECW 28, pp. 43–4. Althusser identifies what is often considered to be the introduction to the *Grundrisse* as the introduction to *A Contribution to the Critique of Political Economy*.

32 'For almost forty years, we have emphasized that the class struggle is the immediate motive force of history.' Marx and Engels, 'Communist Manifesto', MECW 6, pp. 482, 482n; Karl Marx and Friedrich Engels, 'To August Bebel, Wilhelm Liebknecht, Wilhelm Bracke and Others (Circular Letter)', 17–18 September 1879, MECW 45, p. 408.

33 Karl Marx, *A Contribution to the Critique of Political Economy*, Preface, MECW 29, p. 263. The MECW translation reads: 'In the social production of their existence, men inevitably enter into definite relations, which are independent of their will.'

34 Althusser himself translates a good part of the Preface

to *A Contribution* in 'Marx in his Limits', in Althusser, *Philosophy of the Encounter*, pp. 7–162. In his French translation, 'men ... enter into definite relations' becomes, in accordance with what he proposes below, '*les hommes sont partie prenante dans des rapports déterminées*', which might be rendered in English as 'men are a party to determinate relations' ('Marx dans ses limites', in Althusser, *Écrits philosophiques et politiques*, vol. 1, ed. François Matheron [Paris: Stock/Imec, 1994], p. 410).

35 Marx, *A Contribution*, Preface, p. 262 ('appropriate to a given stage in the development of [men's] material forces of production').

36 Untranslatable wordplay. The French word 'correspondance' means not only what its English cognate does, but also 'connection' in the sense in which one says that a traveller 'missed her connection'.

37 Untranslatable wordplay. The expression '*partie prenante*', 'a party to', means, literally, a 'part [that is] taking'. *Prendre*, 'to take', of which *prenant(e)* is the present participle, is the verb Althusser uses in 'On Genesis' and elsewhere to designate the conjoining of elements that can result from an encounter. Thus, one of the meanings of the translation of Marx that Althusser here proposes is that individuals 'take' as agents of the process of production in the wake of their encounter with it.

38 And to labour-power (see *infra*) [Althusser's note].

39 Marx, *A Contribution*, Preface, pp. 263–4.

40 'It is always the direct relationship [*das unmittelbare Verhältnis*] of the owners of the conditions of production to the direct producers ... which reveals the innermost secret, the hidden basis of the entire social structure.' Marx, *Capital Volume Three*, p. 778. The plural form [*Produktionsverhältnisse*] occurs in the sentence immediately preceding the one Althusser cites.

41
$$DP <==> PF \begin{cases} MP \\ \\ LP \end{cases}$$

42 Marx, *Capital Volume Three*, pp. 625–6.

43 Marx, *Capital Volume One*, p. 90; Marx, *Capital Volume Three*, p. 328.

44 See Marx, *Grundrisse*, MECW 28, pp. 399ff; Karl Marx

and Friedrich Engels, *Pre-Capitalist Economic Formations* (Moscow: International Publishers, 1972).

45 Marx, 'Chapter Six: Results of the Direct Production Process', pp. 392, 397, 405, 420, 431.

46 Evgeny Pashukanis, *Law and Marxism, A General Theory: Toward a Critique of the Fundamental Juridical Concepts*, trans. B. Einhorn (London: Ink Links, 1978).

47 See Louis Althusser, *On the Reproduction of Capitalism*, pp. 164ff.

48 Althusser, *For Marx*, pp. 237–8; Althusser, 'The Object of *Capital*', p. 291.

49 Lucien Sève, *Marxisme et théorie de la personnalité* (Paris: Éditions sociales, 1972), p. 97n. In this long note, Sève develops a critique of Althusser's theses on Marx's 'theoretical anti-humanism'.

50 The *sic* is Althusser's.

51 Marx et al., *The German Ideology*, p. 522; Marx, *Economic Manuscript of 1861–1863 (Conclusion)*, MECW 34, p. 89.

52 First version: 'the return of classical bourgeois ideology, defined by Locke, in Marxism'.

53 Karl Marx, Letter of 5 March 1852 to Joseph Weydemeyer, MECW 39, p. 62.

54 Althusser's barb is aimed above all at the Trotskyist Ligue communiste révolutionnaire.

55 Section 10 begins on page 72.

56 Nicolas Malebranche, *The Search after Truth* and *Elucidations of The Search after Truth*, trans. and eds. T.M. Lennon and Paul J. Olscamp (Columbus, OH: Ohio State University Press, 1980), p. 161.

57 Immanuel Kant, *Metaphysics of Morals*, trans. Mary Gregor (New York: Cambridge University Press, 2001), §13, pp. 83–4.

58 If one is intent on finding, at all costs, a type of individual at the origins of the capitalist mode of production, it is by no means the *direct* independent petty producer, but the one whom Marx calls 'moneybags' or 'the owner of money' [*l'homme aux écus*], who is precisely not a direct producer, not even a petty direct producer, but a non-producer, a man who, by a thousand different means, usury or trade in stolen goods and the like, has accumulated a fund of cash which he will use as money-capital to buy a building and

set 'artisans' of the earliest form of manufacture up in it, providing them with the raw material he purchases as well as ad hoc tools.

'Moneybags' is the 'bearer' of primitive accumulation, a social function 'shared out' among a certain number of individuals. Thus, it is primitive accumulation that is 'at the origin' of capitalism: it is not its origin, but *one of the conditions* of its emergence, to which one must also add the existence, on a social scale, of 'free labourers', 'free' of any and all means of production.

Let us note – this is crucial – that once the capitalist relation of production has been constituted in a social formation, constituted and incarnated in it, the capitalist mode of production has still not been assured *of existing* and developing. It is not known – that is, one *does not care to know* – that before existing in the form familiar to us, the Western (English, French and so on) historical form, the capitalist mode of production was born, constituted itself, saw a certain development highly advanced in its forms (including a task-based labour process and assembly-line work), and then *died* in certain fourteenth-century Northern Italian cities (the length of the Po). That a mode of production can die after being born, that the capitalist mode of production can die, can have died several times after being born – what a scandal! For, by common consent, it can die only in order to yield to socialism. Simply, it disappeared from the social formation that had been its support. For that social formation took the form of a city. What was required was the nation (Machiavelli). [Althusser's note] See Marx, *Capital Volume One*, pp. 707–8, 707n; Friedrich Engels, 'To the Italian Reader' (Preface to the Italian edition of the *Communist Manifesto*), MECW 27, p. 366.

59 See above, n. 43.
60 Marx, *Capital Volume One*, pp. 707ff, 713, 713n.
61 See Louis Althusser, 'Notes, hypothèses et interrogations sur le problème du "développement rural" en Afrique', Imec, Althusser Fonds, Alt2.A7–01.01.
62 Marx, *Capital Volume One*, pp. 704ff.
63 Karl Marx, 'The British Rule in India', MECW 12, pp. 126–33; Karl Marx, 'The Future Results of British Rule in India', MECW 12, pp. 217–22.

64   Marx, *Capital Volume Three*, pp. 332, 773; Karl Marx, *Economic Manuscript of 1861–63: A Contribution to the Critique of Political Economy*, MECW 33, p. 20.

65   Karl Marx, 'Marx to Vera Zasulich in Geneva', Letter of 8 March 1881, MECW 46, pp. 71–2; Marx, 'Drafts of the correspondence with Vera Zasulich', MECW 24, pp. 346–69.

66   Vladimir Lenin, *The Development of Capitalism in Russia*, LCW 3, pp. 26–8, 82ff, 166, 185–6; Vladimir Lenin, 'Narodism and the Class of Wage-Workers', LCW 20, pp. 105–8.

67   Kautsky, *The Agrarian Question*, vol. 2, pp. 339ff.

68   Marx et al., *The German Ideology*, pp. 64ff, 76; Marx and Engels, 'Communist Manifesto', pp. 488–9, 505; Marx, *Capital Volume One*, p. 357. See also Friedrich Engels [and Karl Marx], *Anti-Dühring: Herr Eugen Dühring's Revolution in Science*, MECW 25, pp. 282ff.

69   There are three drafts of this text in Althusser's archives. The first bears the same title as the Introduction (not reproduced in the present volume) – 'Towards Imperialism's Final Crisis' – and was probably meant to be integrated into it. Another version, three sentences long, is untitled. A third version is included in a chapter titled 'On State Monopoly Capitalism'. Only the first sentence of the text presented here comes from the untitled version; the rest is based on 'Towards Imperialism's Final Crisis'.

70   'Extracts from the Statement of the Conference of Eighty-one Communist and Workers' Parties, Moscow, 6 December 1960', *Documents on International Affairs, 1960*, eds. Richard Gott, John Major and Geoffrey Warner (London: Oxford University Press, 1964), p. 223.

71   Baruch Spinoza, *Theological-Political Treatise*, ed. Seymour Feldman, trans. Samuel Shirley (Indianapolis, IN: Hackett, 1998 [Gebhardt edition, 1925]), p. 179.

72   Karl Marx, *Grundrisse*, Introduction, MECW 28, pp. 475, 478; Marx, *Capital Volume One*, pp. 317ff, 588ff; Marx, *Capital Volume Three*, pp. 207–8, 229–30, 654, 839ff. See also Roger Establet, 'Presentation of the Plan of *Capital*', in *Reading Capital*, pp. 514–19, 529–30.

73   Karl Marx, 'Value, Prices, Profit', MECW 20, pp. 147–9;

Capital Volume Three, pp. 209ff. See also *Grundrisse*, MECW 29, pp. 130ff.

74 In the manuscript, one finds 'mt', which, in Althusser's manuscripts, usually means 'movement'. He may have meant to write 'manifestation' here.

75 Marx, *Capital Volume One*, pp. 565ff; Marx, *Capital Volume Three*, pp. 779–80. See also *Grundrisse*, MECW 28, p. 208.

76 Marx, *Capital Volume One*, pp. 177ff, pp. 399, 570.

77 Untranslatable wordplay. The French word for duck, *canard*, also means false note.

78 The governmental programme of the French Communist Party, the Socialist Party and the Left Radicals, signed by the Communists and Socialists in June 1972 and the Left Radicals the following September.

79 This slogan, which the French Communist Party put in circulation some time before the Common Programme was signed, was supposed to characterize the regime that the Union of the Left would establish during the transition to socialism. Georges Séguy (see above, n. 25) described the new democracy as 'a progressive democracy that would administer public affairs in the interests of the people and under its real control'. Séguy, 'Answer to question 6', in *Georges Séguy répond à 20 questions*, Supplement to *Vie ouvrière*, 1377 (20 January 1971).

80 Aristotle, *Ethica Nicomachea (Nicomachean Ethics)*, trans. W.D. Ross, in *The Basic Works of Aristotle*, ed. Richard McKeon (New York: Random House, 1941) pp. 1004–11; *Politics*, trans. Benjamin Jowett, in ibid., pp. 1135–42.

81 G.W.F. Hegel, *Science of Logic*, ed. H.D. Lewis, trans. A.V. Miller (Atlantic Highlands, NJ: Humanities Paperback Library, 1969), pp. 139ff.

82 Thomas Hobbes, *Leviathan*, eds. A.P. Martinich and Brian Battiste (London: Broadview, 2011), p. 125.

83 'A veritable freemason society vis-à-vis the whole working class.' Marx, *Capital Volume Three*, p. 197.

84 See above, n. 72.

85 'What is "familiarly known" is not properly known, just for the reason that it is "familiar"'. G.W.F. Hegel, *The Phenomenology of Mind*, trans. J.B. Baillie (New York: Humanities Press, 2nd edn, 1977), p. 92.

86   Vladimir Lenin, *Imperialism, the Highest Stage of Capitalism: A Popular Outline*, LCW 22, p. 187.
87   Империализм как высшая стадия капитализма. This is the title under which the text was published in the USSR from 1920 on, usually translated into English as 'imperialism, the highest stage of capitalism'.
88   Империализм как новейший этап капитализма.
89   Lenin, *Imperialism, the Highest Stage of Capitalism*, pp. 276ff.
90   See above, n. 1.
91   *Faire marcher notre tête*: A watchword that Georges Marchais, General Secretary of the French Communist Party at the time, addressed to Party militants in 1973.
92   Jean-Jacques Rousseau, *Emile, or Education*, Book III, trans. Barbara Foxley, Indianapolis, IN: The Online Library of Liberty, 2011, http://oll.libertyfund.org/titles/rousseau-emile-or-education/simple#lf1499-head-009.   (Althusser's quotation is inexact; Rousseau writes 'je me laisse quelques fois entraîner à la force des conséquences'/'I sometimes let myself be carried away by the strength of consequences').
93   Marx, *A Contribution*, Preface, p. 265. These are the last lines of the Preface.
94   Both translations are found in the manuscript.
95   'As [men completely ignorant of the existing economical system] now defend the "eternity" of capital rule [*sic*; Marx wrote this text in English] and the wages system, if they had lived in feudal times or in times of slavery, they would have defended the feudal system and the slave system as founded on the nature of things, as springing from nature.' Karl Marx, 'First Draft of the Civil War in France', MECW, vol. 22, p. 504. See also *Capital Volume One*, p. 92.
96   Karl Marx, Letter of 28 December 1846 to Pavel Vasilyevich Annenkov, MECW 38, pp. 97, 100; Marx, *Grundrisse*, MECW 29, pp. 209–11; Marx, *Capital Volume One*, pp. 18ff, 587; Marx, *Capital Volume Three*, pp. 240, 258, 626.
97   'The rich man, goaded by necessity, eventually conceived of the shrewdest scheme ever to enter the human mind: to employ on his behalf the very forces of his attackers, to make his opponents his defenders.' Jean-Jacques Rousseau, *Discourse on the Origin of Inequality*, ed. Patrick Coleman,

trans. Franklin Philip (Oxford: Oxford University Press, 2009), p. 68.

98 The *'sic'* is Althusser's.

99 Vladimir Lenin, *Imperialism, The Highest Stage of Capitalism*, p. 194; 'The Impending Catastrophe and How to Combat It', LCW 25, pp. 361–3 (*antichambre* in the French translation corresponds to 'eve' or 'threshold' in the English translation); Vladimir Lenin, *'Left-Wing' Childishness and the Petty-Bourgeois Mentality*, LCW 27, pp. 341–2, 351; Vladimir Lenin, 'Tax in Kind, Freedom to Trade and Concessions', LCW 32, pp. 336–8.

100 See above, n. 71.

101 See above, n. 72.

102 Louis Althusser, 'Reply to John Lewis', in *Essays in Self-Criticism*, pp. 49–50. First published in July 1973, this text was written in summer 1972.

103 Vladimir Lenin, 'International Socialist Congress in Stuttgart', LCW 13, p. 77; Vladimir Lenin, 'The Discussion on Self-Determination Summed Up', LCW 22, p. 343; Lenin, *Imperialism, the Highest Stage of Capitalism*, pp. 278–85, 301–2.

104 Compare Louis Althusser, *Socialisme idéologique et socialisme scientifique* (1966–1967), Imec, Fonds Althusser, Alt2.A8–02.02, p. 82. 'Modes of production are not "transformed"; *social formations* and social formations alone undergo transformation.'

105 Marx and Engels, 'Communist Manifesto', pp. 488, 502–3; *The German Ideology*, pp. 52, 73; Karl Marx, Letter of 28 December 1846 to Pavel Vasilyevich Annenkov, p. 98; Karl Marx, '[On Poland] [Speech at the International Meeting Held in London on 29 November 1847', MECW 6, pp. 388–9. It is not at all clear that Marx consistently took the position that Althusser here attributes to him.

106 Vladimir Lenin, 'The War and Russian Social-Democracy', LCW 21, pp. 32–3; Vladimir Lenin, 'The Revolutionary Proletariat and the Right of Nations to Self-Determination', ibid., pp. 413–14; Lenin, 'The Discussion on Self-Determination Summed Up', LCW 22, pp. 324–5, 339, 346–7; Vladimir Lenin, 'The Tasks of the Proletariat in our Revolution', LCW 24, p. 73.

107 First version: 'that had to be created'.

108 Marx, *A Contribution*, Preface, p. 263. 'No social formation is ever destroyed before all the productive forces for which it is sufficient have been developed.'

109 Friedrich Engels, 'Principles of Communism', MECW 6, p. 349; Marx and Engels, 'Communist Manifesto', p. 489; Marx, *Capital Volume Three*, pp. 249, 261 and note, 248, 258, 439.

110 The manuscript reads 'communism'.

111 Vladimir Lenin, 'The State and Revolution', LCW 25, pp. 475ff; Lenin, 'A Great Beginning', pp. 411–12; Vladimir Lenin, 'Eleventh Congress of the Russian Communist Party (B), March 27–April 2, 1922', LCW 33, pp. 278ff, 310ff.

112 Vladimir Lenin, 'The Junius Pamphlet', LCW 22, pp. 309–10; Vladimir Lenin, 'The New Economic Policy and the Tasks of the Political Education Departments', LCW 33, p. 66; Vladimir Lenin, 'Notes of a Publicist: Without Metaphors,' LCW 33, pp. 206–7; Lenin, 'Eleventh Congress of the R.C.P. (B)', pp. 266–7.

113 See above, n. 40.

114 'The world is all that is the case'. Ludwig Wittgenstein, *Tractatus Logico-philosophicus*, trans. D.F. Pears and B. F. McGuinness (London: Routledge & Kegan Paul, 1976), p. 5.

115 'Elle n'est pas morte' [It isn't dead] (1886), a song about the Paris Commune. The lyrics were written by Eugène Pottier, author of the 'Internationale'; the melody was composed by Victor Parizot.

116 Lenin is supposed to have danced on the snow after Russia's revolutionary government had held power for seventy-three days, one day longer than the Paris Commune.

117 The sentence Althusser cites comes from a proclamation that Charles de Gaulle wrote on 18 June 1940, the day he read, on the BBC, an appeal to the French to continue the war against Germany after the 1940 defeat. The proclamation appeared on a poster signed by de Gaulle and distributed in London and other English cities in June and July. See Charles de Gaulle, 'Nothing is Lost: London, 18 June 1940', in *The Speeches of General de Gaulle* (New York: Oxford University Press, 1944), pp. 1–2.

118 Vladimir Lenin, 'Preface to the Russian Translation of Karl Marx's Letters to Dr. Kugelmann', LCW 12, pp. 109ff;

Vladimir Lenin, 'Lessons of the Commune', LCW 13, p. 477–8.

119 Giulio Cerreti, *À l'ombre des deux T: Quarante ans avec Palmiro Togliatti et Maurice Thorez* (Paris: Julliard, 1973), pp. 50ff, 59ff, 68ff.

120 In July 1931, at the instigation of the Soviet Communist Party leadership, Henri Barbé and Pierre Célor were charged with having created a 'faction' in the French Party's Political Bureau. They were expelled from the Political Bureau soon after. See Louis Althusser, 'On the Twenty-Second Congress of the French Communist Party', trans. Ben Brewster, *New Left Review*, no. 104 (July–August 1977), p. 21, where Barbé and Célor are associated with the 'authoritarianism' of the French Party in the period of 'class against class'.

121 In the wake of the 1927 expulsion of Trotsky and Bukharin from the Soviet Party, the Communist Parties of the Third International adopted an ultrasectarian political line, attacking Social-Democrats and Socialists as 'social fascists', 'the bourgeoisie's best allies during capitalism's final crisis'. Under the slogan 'class against class', the French Party waged a fiercely anti-socialist campaign in the 1927 legislative elections. The Party maintained its sectarian line until the beginning of the Popular Front period in May 1934.

122 Cerreti, *À l'ombre des deux T*, p. 70.

123 'A French comrade – the secretary of a Federation – had, speaking before the Central Committee in 1972, bewailed the fact that, in the elections, the Party kept butting up against a "buffer" (like the ones in stations where trains end): "up to twenty-one percent, but no further"'. Louis Althusser, 'Lettre aux camarades italiens du 28 juillet 1986', Imec, Althusser Fonds, Alt2.A29.06–10. The Italian Communist Party's 'buffer' in the early 1970s was around twenty-seven percent.

124 Cerreti, *À l'ombre des deux T*, pp. 49, 57–8.

125 Vladimir Lenin, LCW 9, pp. 100, 118, 150; LCW 13, pp. 115–16, 128; LCW 15, p. 56; LCW 25, pp. 430–1; LCW 29, p. 381; LCW 30, pp. 262ff, 413–14; LCW 32, pp. 21, 429ff, etc.

126 'By around 1934, it had become impossible and even absurd to think that the work of leadership could be carried out from a single centre' (my translation). Palmiro Togliatti,

'La via italiana al socialismo' (1956), in *Opere*, ed. Luciano Gruppi (Rome: Editori riuniti/Istituto Gramsci, 1984), vol. 4, part 2, pp. 155–9. See Togliatti, 'Alcuni problemi della storia dell'Internazionale communista' (1959), in ibid., vol. 6, p. 401, and Togliatti, 'Interview with *Nuovi Argomenti* (1956)', in Togliatti, *On Gramsci and Other Writings*, ed. Donald Sassoon (London: Lawrence and Wishart, 1979), p. 141.

127 Marx, *Grundrissse*, MECW 29, pp. 134ff; Marx, *Capital Volume Three*, pp. 230ff.

128 *Quotations from Chairman Mao Tse-Tung*, ed. Stuart R. Schram (New York: Frederick A. Praeger, 1967), p. 110 (自力更生，艰苦奋斗).

129 Marx, *Capital Volume Three*, p. 207. In the passage Althusser probably has in mind, the MECW translation of *Kerngestalt* is 'inner pattern'. Elsewhere in MECW, it is translated as 'internal structure' (*Capital Volume Three*, p. 168) or 'inner essence' (ibid., p. 242).

130 Ibid., p. 818.

131 Ibid., p. 27; cf. Karl Marx, Preface to *Capital Volume Three*, *Marx/Engels Gesamtausgabe*, Section 2, vol. 4, Part 2, text, ed. Manfred Müller et al. (Berlin and Amsterdam: Dietz/Internationales Institut für Sozialgeschichte, 1992), p. 7.

Marx and History

1 *'Capital, Volume Four'* is *Theories of Surplus Value*.

2 Marx, *A Contribution*, Preface, p. 263. The corresponding terms in the MECW translation are 'economic structure' and 'superstructure'.

3 See Louis Althusser, *Machiavelli and Us*, ed. François Matheron, trans. Gregory Elliott (London: Verso, 1999), pp. 23–4.

4 Althusser is most likely thinking of Marx's 18 March 1872 letter to the publisher of the French translation of *Capital Volume One*. 'The method of analysis I have used [is] a method not previously applied to economic subjects.' Karl Marx, 'To Citizen Maurice La Châtre', MECW 44, p. 344. Cf. Marx's description of his *dialectical* method in *Capital Volume One*, Afterword to the second German edition, p. 19.

5 Ibid., p. 17, trans. modified.

6 Previous version: 'and communist'.

7 Marx, *A Contribution*, Preface, p. 263.

8 Previous version: 'Obviously, however, there are several ways of conceiving this idea when it is brought into relation with the succession of modes of production cited a moment ago.'

9 Karl Marx, *The Eighteenth Brumaire of Louis Bonaparte*, MECW 11, p. 185.

10 Marx, *Grundrisse*, Introduction, MECW 28, p. 42.

11 Previous version: 'the result of the past'.

12 Marx, *Grundrisse*, Introduction, MECW 28, pp. 42–3. The English translation reads 'the feudal, ancient, and oriental economies'. The German is *Ökonomie* (Karl Marx, 'Einleitung zur Kritik der politischen Ökonomie', *Marx-Engels-Werke* (Berlin: Dietz, 1961), vol. 13, p. 637).

13 Ibid., pp. 39, 43ff.

14 Ibid., p. 42.

15 Ibid. See Althusser, 'The Object of *Capital*', pp. 66–7; Louis Althusser, 'The Humanist Controversy', in *The Humanist Controversy and Other Writings*, pp. 295–6.

16 'The mere result attained [is not] the concrete whole itself, but the result along with the process of arriving at it'. Hegel, *The Phenomenology of Mind*, p. 69. See Louis Althusser, 'On Content in the Thought of G.W.F. Hegel', in Althusser, *The Spectre of Hegel: Early Writings* (London: Verso, 1997), pp. 36, 39, 68.

17 'What is called historical development rests, in general, on the fact that the latest form regards the earlier ones as stages leading towards itself'. Marx, *Grundrisse*, Introduction, MECW 28, pp. 42–3. See also Marx, *Capital Volume One*, p. 707 and Karl Marx, 'Letter to *Otechestvenniye Zapiski*', MECW 24, pp. 200–1.

18 Previous version: 'With a very important reservation that I shall make later, this idea introduces us …'.

19 Marx, *The Poverty of Philosophy*, p. 174.

20 Previous version: 'All the forms of drudgery and all the wars.'

21 Previous version: 'contingency: dominated by the necessity of a tendential mechanism'.

22 In place of this and the preceding paragraph, an earlier

version contains the following passage: 'Here I must confine myself to generalities. I leave the question of universal history aside: Marx shows that history does not possess unity as history and that it ceases to take the form of local, discontinuous histories only when, with capitalism, the material and social unity of a world market comes into existence. I come now to the implantation of history in a historical human group, a social formation.'

23 Immanuel Kant, 'Lectures on Pedagogy', trans. Robert B. Louden, in Kant, *Anthropology, History, and Education*, eds. Louden and Günter Zöller (Cambridge: Cambridge University Press, 2007), p. 460.

24 Cited in Thomas Bentley, *Letters on the Utility and Policy of Employing Machines to Shorten Labour* (London: William Sleater, 1780), pp. 2–3.

25 Marx, *Capital Volume One*, p. 331n4.

26 Previous version: 'to ensure reproduction'.

27 Marx, *Grundrisse*, Introduction, MECW 28, p. 42.

28 See n. 1 to 'Book on Imperialism'.

29 'Archimedes sought but one firm and immovable point in order to move the entire earth from one place to another. Just so, great things are also to be hoped for if I succeed in finding just one thing, however slight, that is certain and unshaken.' René Descartes, *Meditations, Objections, and Replies*, eds. and trans. Roger Ariew and Donald Cress (Indianapolis, IN: Hackett, 2006), p. 13.

On History

1 See Althusser, 'On the Objectivity of History', p. 7.

2 In the handwritten manuscript, there are underlined blanks representing the words 'the theory' after the two occurrences of 'as'.

3 See Althusser, *How to Be a Marxist in Philosophy*, pp. 87–8.

4 Ibid., p. 138; Althusser, *Philosophy for Non-Philosophers*, pp. 97–8; Althusser, *Les Vaches noires*, p. 190.

Index